Diary of a Publicity Guru!

The 'Glitzy' World of promoting the Post Office

Paul Diggens has had extensive experience in many of life's roles - as a pirate radio operator, a clerk in the Telephone Manager's Office, a journalist and press officer with the Post Office and for many years Head of PR & Media. In the early years working as a clerk he was told that the Post Office were looking for young men with new ideas to promote what was an old-fashioned civil service organization that was stuck in the past. In *Diary of a Publicity Guru* we are taken into the world-class glitzy milieu of media and promotional events with many personalities, staff, children and animals covering some of the world's most inane subjects.

By the same Author -

Amphigouri a comedy of errors for laughter

Diary of a Publicity Guru
The 'Glitzy' World of promoting the Post Office

Paul Diggens

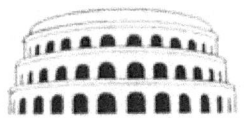

Arena Books

Copyright © Paul Diggens 2020

The right of Paul Diggens to be identified as author of this book has been asserted in accordance with the Copyright, Designs and Patents Act 1988. All characters and events described in this book are fictional and any resemblance to actual persons, living or dead, is purely coincidental.

First published in 2020 by Arena Books

Arena Books
6 Southgate Green
Bury St. Edmunds
IP33 2BL

www.arenabooks.co.uk

Distributed in America by Ingram International, One Ingram Blvd., P.O. Box 3006, La Vergne, TN 37086-1985, USA.

All rights reserved. Except for the quotation of short passages for the purposes of criticism and review, no part of this publication may be reproduced, stored in a retrieval system, or transmitted, in any form or by any means, electronic, mechanical, photocopying, recording or otherwise, without the prior permission of the author or the publisher acting as his agent.

Paul Diggens
Diary of a Publicity Guru *the 'Glitzy' World of promoting the Post Office*

British Library cataloguing in Publication Data. A Catalogue record for this book is available from the British Library.

ISBN-13   978-1-911593-70-6

BIC classifications:- BGA, BGB, KJD, KJH.

Cover design
By Jason Anscomb

Typeset in
Times New Roman

CONTENTS

FOREWORD		page -	9
Chapter 1	The Postcode Sensation		11
Chapter 2	Postal Reps and Mail Coaches		21
Chapter 3	Start of the Flying Postie		30
Chapter 4	The Postbus the Detector Vans and the Bug		39
Chapter 5	Animals, History, and the Blue Dot Experience		50
Chapter 6	Poco Balloon Races and the Golden Hinde		61
Chapter 7	Postman Pat and other Personalities		76
Chapter 8	Crime Stamps and Transport		82
Chapter 9	Poco's Postbus and Concorde		88
Chapter 10	The Glitz of the VSOE		93
Chapter 11	Diversifications		99
Chapter 12	Promotions to the Forefront		106
Chapter 13	Poco's Postcode Song & more Stamps		117
Chapter 14	Canal Post Office and Gallantry Stamps		127
Chapter 15	New look to Christmas		131
Chapter 16	The National Lottery and the Post Office		136
Chapter 17	Animals Again		141
Chapter 18	Creating even more Media		151
Chapter 19	End of 20th Century Highlights		163
Chapter 20	Thank you and Farewell ?		197

FOREWORD

This is the story, spanning over 30 years, of Paul Robert Diggens in the Public Relations Department of The Post Office.

The book is illustrated with picture caption stories, in the true form of media press releases of its time. The journey begins in the 1970s through to the Year 2000. These are the days of 'the-end-of-the-gin-and-tonic-man' for, during the early days of PR, all problems seemed to be solved with a G&T! This was a time when the Post Office was looking for young executives with new ideas – perchance to bring it from the old Civil Service times, into a more modern era.

Left to right: The late Joe Cantley, Director, Eastern Postal Region, Celebrated actress Sally Thomsett and Mr Public Relations Department – Paul Robert Diggens, author of this fleeting glimpse into Post Office PR.

As in introduction into the glizy world of promoting the Post Office - The British Pullman Carriages of the Venice Simplon Orient Express provided a great opportunity for Sally Thomsett of the Railway Children, to join us on our special trip to Cromer, to donate an inshore lifeboat to the local RNLI; until the late 1950s the railway delivered lifeboats free of charge to seaside locations for the RNLI. A special stamp issue of 'Lifeboats' necessitated an excuse to spend some money for marketing … or for a 'jolly'. It was 1987 and Post Office Marketing was new, with Area Marketing Managers wooing businesses to use postal services – but there was little competition in those days – so a 'jolly' day out was had by all with local and regional newspaper competition winners to boot. During the 1970s, '80s and '90s, 'jollies' were big business in PR. More about the day's activities in the 1980 chapters!

Chapter 1
The Postcode Sensation

So, it all began back in the 1970s. Postcodes are naturally given today but, when they were introduced initially in Norwich (as, say, Anglia TV's address of NOR 07A) Joe Public did not take easily to adding it to addresses on envelopes, etc. – so campaigns were launched by the Post Office to educate and train.

A silver postal van at Cambridge raised the game in promoting the use of postcodes. The original Norwich trial failed, so postcodes were reviewed and re-formatted in order to make them more electronically recognizable on envelopes – NOR became NR and some 24 million addresses in the UK were given a postcode. But how would the public remember to use them? What could be done to get the message over? Who, or what, could be used to promote this address element?

1970s – It's the 'Use Your Postcode' Era.

DIARY OF A PUBLICITY GURU

Children from a local school in Cambridge City Centre with the new Postcode publicity silver van.

Poco the postcode elephant was born – he came in many shapes and forms being re-drawn to a young and more acceptable image as the years progressed!

DIARY OF A PUBLICITY GURU

Life at the Essex County Show on the Post Office stand.

Relaxing in a bath one day back in the early '70s, I remembered the adage 'an elephant never forgets' ... so why not invent an elephant who never forgets to use his postcode? Thus, Poco the postcode elephant was born – firstly a sticker – Poco says "Don't Forget Your Postcode" then, as it was county show-time, a walking and a talking elephant were introduced.

The talking elephant was star of many shows – it was fitted with a sensor, so anyone walking past it would activate the recording and the head and trunk would move. Much fun at the Royal Norfolk Show – it had a real Norfolk person with a strong accent to make a special recording ... "Have you got a postcode? Of course, you have!"

The then Lord Mayor of Norwich and his wife (she had had a few glasses!) toured the Post Office stand and, as she walked past Poco, got a huge shock as his voice boomed out. She almost jumped out of her skin and used her handbag to assault the elephant, using a few expletives in the process.

Another Poco element at the county shows was the walking elephant that gave rides on its howdah.

Just look at how the DIY county show stand was …

The Royal Norfolk Show Post Office Stand.

Home-made stand? I think so! A lorry and exhibition caravan with a tarpaulin between, was how the Post Office met and portrayed itself to the public and its numerous customers. However, the greatest element of the show stand was the free rides on Poco – but how did it work and where did it come from?

Back after war-time Britain, several mechanical elephants were operated on the nation's beaches. One such elephant was kept for many years at a village near Chelmsford and the PR crew would hire it from the start of the show season, through the summer from May to September, before the motor transport department took it apart to repair it and then suggested a project to build one.

Beneath the howdah was a lawn-mower engine with drive belts to the wheels under the legs, the accelerator was behind its ear and the head turned to move Poco around in a large circle – it even went backwards.

There was much fun at the Essex County Show when it got a puncture. I proceeded to the AA Stand as a rescue job to enquire if they could help. Speaking to a senior AA engineer, I said my elephant had a puncture and would they come and repair it?

DIARY OF A PUBLICITY GURU

The response was: "I think you must have been drinking with the Young Farmers – will you kindly leave our stand? "Pursuing the request, I said that I really did have an elephant with a puncture, but the response was the same.

However, I managed to persuade another engineer to have a look – and … success! The puncture was repaired … and a picture of the repair job made it into the AA monthly publication. The engineer said: "By God, you *do* have an elephant with a puncture – in my 40 years in the AA, I have never repaired an elephant!"

Poco was moved from show to show in a horsebox, pulled by a Royal Mail exhibition vehicle. Poco travelled throughout London, East Anglia and the South East.

After a show in Kent, Poco was hauled back to Colchester through central London where there had been a jewelry raid. Just imagine the scene – police barriers stopping and investigating all the traffic, checking all drivers and vehicles … and a long traffic jam. Poco moved along and eventually reached the front of the queue being held up by two police officers.

"Ok, let's have a look in your cab," they said, "where have you come from and where are you going to? And what's in your trailer?"

"An elephant," we said.

"Oh yes," they said, "what have you really got in the trailer?"

"An elephant," we said, "take a look."

"Let's all look," said the police officers … so we did.

Opening the trailer, a gasp – "You *do* have an elephant!"

Then they went inside the trailer and checked Poco's trunk … just in case the diamonds were hidden there!

Needless to say – they were not!

The new Poco under construction.

DIARY OF A PUBLICITY GURU

There was always an angle for postcodes as they affected everyone ... Mr Postcode – the man who created your postcode from your address ...

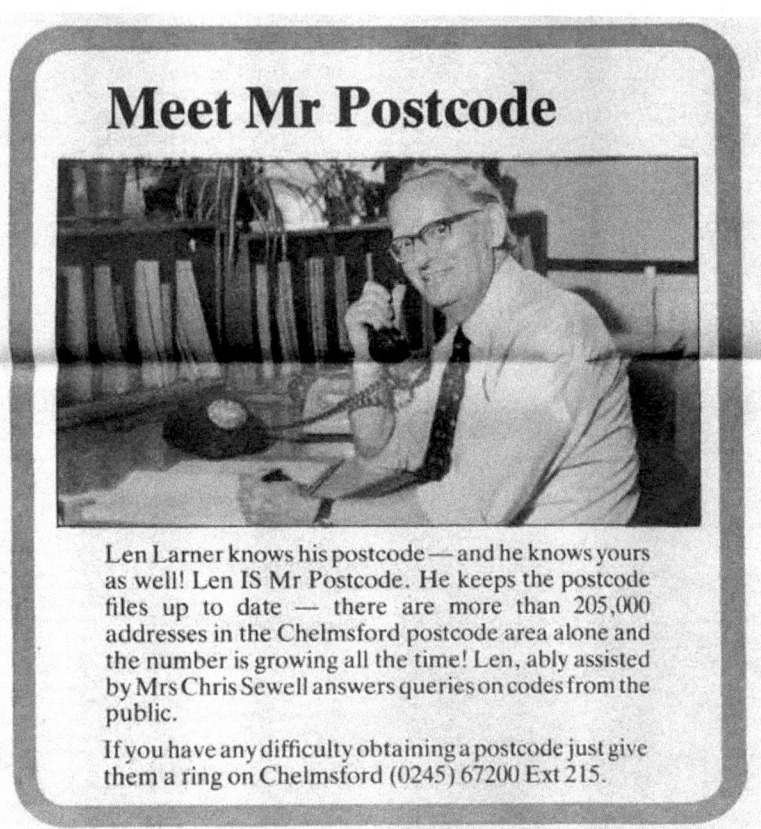

Meet Mr Postcode

Len Larner knows his postcode — and he knows yours as well! Len IS Mr Postcode. He keeps the postcode files up to date — there are more than 205,000 addresses in the Chelmsford postcode area alone and the number is growing all the time! Len, ably assisted by Mrs Chris Sewell answers queries on codes from the public.

If you have any difficulty obtaining a postcode just give them a ring on Chelmsford (0245) 67200 Ext 215.

Glamour of publicity? Not always – taking postcode exhibitions around the country they had to be moved on a Saturday night to the next town. Well remember turning up at Bletchley Milton Keynes to set up the exhibition only to find that the engineers had not connect the electric to the portable tenting building – so lorry to unload and exhibition to set up in the dark except for the headlights of the car and lorry – great fun !!

Miss Postcode draws a lucky winning ticket.

Miss Postcode – looking good in the latest C&A fashions we bought from the local store … or the girl in the tele-ad department of the local paper, who managed to get more postcodes in her ads than everyone else that week and won a clothes voucher!

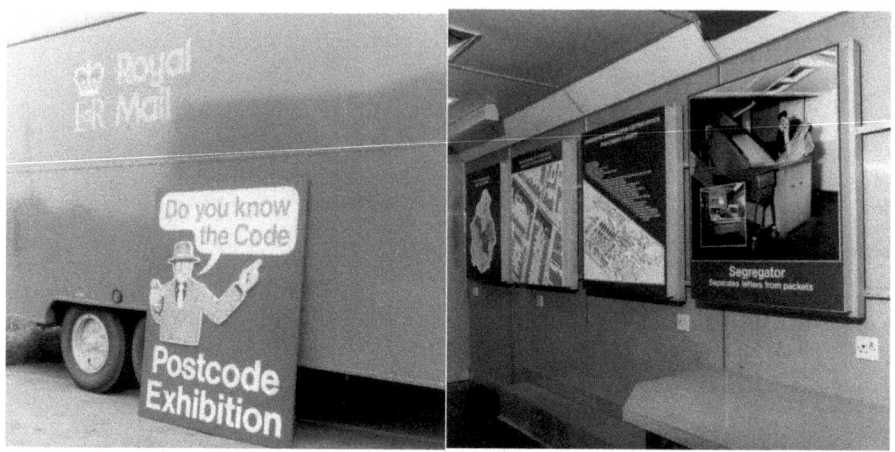

Postcode promotions – always lots to do to educate the nation. But more about Poco in the 1980s with his fan club and 45 rpm record later ……

Chapter 2
Postal Reps and Mail coaches

Alongside postcode promotions came the postal services reps and every Head Post Office area had one like the Colchester one above. A fleet of 'reps' cars were purchased – red naturally – and postal marketing began.

Was 'Store to Door' the advance of Amazon many years earlier?

Philately was big business in those lazy hazy days of the '70s, but the display and exhibition units lacked finesse. Storvider Pan Focal – wooden panels with steel couplings seemed the best on offer, or Marler Haley plastic clips panels for smaller runs.

DIARY OF A PUBLICITY GURU

Promoting stamp collecting in the 1970s was also fun. Regional and local newspapers had an appetite of competitions to attract readers and, indeed, to use up space in the pagination of their publications, so line drawings for stamp colouring competitions always went down well.

Coach-and-four in the streets of Bedford.

Major media events always involved post office history of delivering the mail over the years and mail coach props always gathered big crowds – especially if there were add-ons.

A mail coach-and-four always necessitated good planning with trips to London for props. In north-west London, Bapty & Co. could supply a brace of pistols, blunderbuss, sword and cutlass for the mail guard; Berman and Angels would supply the mail guard costume.

The add-ons were good value. I well remember at Angels being accosted by a large wardrobe department lady … "You put that jacket on – yes, you are about the size of the big Ronnie, that'll fit him." She must have been from the BBC!

Then we had a highwayman hidden away somewhere en-route to hold up the coach and take the guests to ransom, such as the Mayor or Mayoress of the town. This was a good photo opportunity … especially if the Mayor had to give up his wallet. In Norwich, at one such event, the Lord Mayor nearly fainted when 'held-up' as he thought the highwayman was for real.

The mail coaches of their time were regularly held up by highwaymen. In fact, the last highwayman to be publicly hanged by the post office has his grave just outside Hemel Hempstead. It's among four trees that are between the railway and the road where Robert Snooks has his resting place at Boxmoor.

DIARY OF A PUBLICITY GURU

He held up a post boy who was taking mail from Tring to Hemel Hempstead on Sunday, 10th May 1801.

The following day Postmaster and High Constable of the Kings Arms at Berkhamsted, John Page, initiated enquires and folk came forward to say they had seen a man with a horse just before the crime. Snooks was an ostler at the Kings Arms and knew of the post boy's route.

A reward was offered for apprehending this man who was later seen and arrested in Marlborough Forest. After his execution, his body was dug up and interred in a coffin provided by the residents of Hemel Hempstead before being re-interred on the moor. A small headstone was erected in 1904 with a footstone installed in 1994. At the time of writing, there is a Snooks Bar for eating and drinking in Hemel Hempstead.

Mail coach days were fun ...

Left: At Stevenage.

Right: At Bedford.

Stand and Deliver!

The mail coach highwayman and/or highwaywoman hold-up!

The Christmas card stagecoach – visiting a care home in Aylesbury where someone was celebrating their 100th birthday.

And a mail coach guard from 1860 wearing a futuristic watch!

The days when Post Office vintage vehicles could be used.

Here at the Royal Norfolk Show, About Anglia (the then Anglia Television news) went 'on-air' live with the presenters starring alongside our vintage replica van from 1910. Vehicles from past eras always made good public interface. With post office history, there was always an excuse for a cavalcade of communication across the years.

Chapter 3
Start of the Flying Postal Services

The 'Flying Postie'

During the late 1970s, the flying postie services were introduced with opportunities to take journalists with the mail. While the days of the travelling post offices were still part and parcel (excuse the pun!), bulk mail could be moved quickly by plane from Norwich, Stansted or Southend, thereby beating the railway by hours. So, firstly, we took journalists to Stansted as a teaser to watch the mail operation. The Stansted Airport PR Executive, Derek Winter, took us on an early evening coach journey around the airport and even along the main runway before the customary nosebag and drinks (meal and booze, of course) and then the mid-evening flight loading.

Standing with his back to the coach windscreen, Derek on mic began his history and operations talk about the airport and we all gained lots of info as the coach turned on the main runway. Derek said that, from time to time, wild deer would cross the runway but none had been seen for some years – only to be accompanied by strong laughter from the assembled guests for, behind him, a small herd of reindeer did actually cross the runway right on cue!

Elderly aircraft and, indeed, elderly crew were involved in the flying postie operation. On a recce at Stansted, I met with the air crew and an elderly pilot – he asked me where the weather office was as he couldn't get hold of them, due to the fact his wireless had stopped working on the plane. Even a small distance away from him, it appeared he had already sampled the duty-frees on his incoming flight. Some weeks later I learned he had been dismissed for operational reasons!

Life above the clouds was not always as glam as expected – sitting on a pile of mail-bags all netted down in case of turbulence and doing some media interviews and tv appearances while feeling a little air-sick wondering if we will actually make it and land in these vintage aircraft !

Some very late nights !.

DIARY OF A PUBLICITY GURU

Flying 'first class' can be uncomfortable

Story by ROBERT HADGRAFT, pictures by JOHN KERR.

A 1948 Dakota heaved its considerable bulk off Norwich Airport runway this week — and signalled the beginning of the festive season!

Christmas may be the best part of four weeks away — but it has already begun for our postmen.

The flood of Christmas mail began this week, triggering off sighs of "here we go again" from sorting offices all over the UK.

But, although the 1979 seasonal mail is expected to be just as heavy as previous years, it will be dealt with this time in a different fashion.

In the summer the Post Office launched its new Royal Mail airlift operation — and now it will really come into its own.

Nerve centre

Mail from East Anglia is involved in this special operation — which has been nicknamed the "Flying Postie."

The scheme focuses on Liverpool's Speke Airport, which acts as the nerve centre for several air routes.

East Anglia's link-up comes via Norwich Airport. The other flights are from Bristol, Newcastle, Glasgow, Cardiff and Lydd in Kent.

The "Flying Postie" is taking over where it proves more efficient than rail links, and carries first class letters and packets only.

Norwich link

East Anglia's mail is transported to Norwich Sorting Office — one of Britain's 36 mechanised offices.

Little Ipswich mail goes to Norwich in this way as rail links from the town are efficient enough not to require the "Flying Postie."

However mail coming to Ipswich is flown in via Norwich.

Michelle

A first class letter posted in Norwich during the evening can now be delivered in Bristol before breakfast.

To ensure maximum publicity for this de-luxe distribution stystem, the Post Office invited pressmen to join the mailbags on a night-flight from Norwich to Liverpool this week.

Thirty-year-old Dakotas are not the most comfortable of planes — and it is also quite rare to come across an air hostess with a Norfolk accent.

Michelle was specially provided by the airline and the Post Office to keep us as comfortable as possible.

However, comfort is not a word that springs to mind when I recall the flight.

But then mailbags don't really need particularly comfortable surroundings.

Teething problems

The Norwich flight is one of seven converging on Speke Airport within a 30 minute period, five nights a week.

Personnel at the airport swap all the bags around and the "old faithfuls" go back to their various airports with mail for their own region.

The whole operation depends upon tight sorting schedules and train links being met and is a carefully calculated scheme.

It has had one or two teething problems, though, as a supervisor at Speke Airport will testify.

He had one or two choice Scouse phrases for the people who don't tell him when flights are cancelled, and for the fog which can put a spanner in the works.

Neverless the Post Office public relations men told us the whole thing has been a huge success — and they brought out the champagne to prove their point.

In fact, the Tuesday night and Wednesday morning link-ups were the first time the "Flying Postie" from Norwich has involved a Dakota DC3.

Normally a tiny aircraft is used. The change was brought into effect for the onset of Christmas mail and the benefit of the TV and pressmen.

The airlift operation will cost the Post Office about £1.8 million over the year — but it says the improvement in customer service fully justified this.

And the "Flying Postie" is carrying 250,000 letters each day. During the Christmas pressure period more than 400,000 items will be carried.

ABOVE: The Eastern Airways DC3 ready to return to Norwich.

ABOVE right: Captain Reg Eames, left, and 1st Officer Jim Cardar who piloted the DC3 "Flying Postie."

RIGHT: Unloading mailbags at Liverpool.

Inland air mail is, of course, not new. Six per cent of first class mail is already carried by air, but until now an extension air service has proved uneconomic over a single route.

The new system has been designed so that aircraft carries a mail load bound for several destinations.

It is an operation signals the start of "Tomorrow's World" the Royal Mail, says the Post Office.

And if that means greater value for the stamp then I'll drink to (even at 6,000 feet).

DIARY OF A PUBLICITY GURU

Not the one-mile high club – but an old Dakota probably from 1942 era – operated by Eastern Airways.

With the mail netted and around 12 journalists safely seated behind the mail, plus hostess Michelle aboard, we took off for Liverpool. BBC Television were also on board and reporter Ian Masters asked me to sit on the mailbags and be interviewed during the flight. We spoke about the slick ground operation of moving the mail for a few minutes, then he slipped in his final question about the age of the aircraft saying, "Will we really make it back with all this weight to land safely in Liverpool?" ... to which I responded, "No problem, but please all keep peddling at the back."

But after a few glasses of 'champoo' and on-board hospitality, we reached Liverpool for a quick turnaround and a midnight take-off back to Norwich. A great clear night and numerous twinkling lights on the ground – however, as we accelerated away, sparks flew out from the engines and I asked hostie Michelle if all was ok? To which she responded in a broad Norfolk accent: "I think something's gone wrong. I wish I was back home in my bed in Norwich."

We landed safely in Norwich 90 minutes later, and a splendid time was had by all.

Press conference airside at Southend Airport.

Flying up to Liverpool with British Air Ferries – again mail netted at the front of the aircraft and 20+ seats at the rear.

A rough night – perchance only freight should fly – and BAF Boss greeted us at the airport saying that it was a pity about the small building at the end of the runway, as we needed clearance between the ground and the aircraft. He explained that, if the building had not been there, we could have carried heavier loads of mail. Then he helpfully added, "We've not had an incident recently and it's probably our turn … perhaps tonight."

So, a rough night and lots of turbulence – one 'stills' photographer had his eyes closed for the entire flight, whilst telling himself he would be alright … but his finger nails were gradually cutting into the back of the hand of his female reporter sitting next to him.

It was an easier flight on return to Southend airport – but again a late night – 2.00am landing and a full day at work later …

Night-life at numerous 'Flying Postie' airports !

Chapter 4
The Postbus the Detector Van the Bug !

A modern 'Constable' in Flatford on the Essex/Suffolk border.

Back in the mid-1960s there was the Jack Report into the rather depleting rural transport network and there was a suggestion that passengers might ride with the mail once again in a modern mail coach.

So, enter the postbus ... many in very rural areas of Scotland but, in East Anglia, services were introduced in the Diss/Gislingham area around the Norfolk and Suffolk county border and, in Essex and Suffolk, Colchester to Dedham and Flatford –John Constable Country. Lots of media interest as passengers and mail travelled together – here at Willy Lott's Cottage, made famous by painter John Constable, this picture was well used.

In fact, a magazine programme of BBC News in East Anglia were to use it on their Friday night 10.00pm programme but – alas! – it went out at the same time as a massive thunderstorm and, in those days of 425 or 605 lines transmissions, the signal was non-existent so this news item was not seen by many viewers.

There was a certain kind of magic with the modern mail coach – passenger numbers increased and postbus societies developed with members visiting postbus sites and taking a ride, asking the drivers many questions and photographing each and every stop. It was at that time the BBC radio programmes featured some unusual trading locations and they chose 'Berney Arms' near Great Yarmouth as a very interesting postal delivery. So with postman and reporter we left on the train to Norwich for the first station – Berney Arms. This station was only served by 2 trains a day so the postman had special timings to do his round. The deliveries were to cottages next to the Broads, remote locations of reed men, the pub and the windmill. Despite every effort to keep to time the BBC reporter strayed from the schedule asking even more questions at the windmill – so much so that we missed the last and only train back to Great Yarmouth. Our only option was to walk along the railway track – this is of course illegal and can generate a fine of trespass on the railway. 105 minutes later, exhausted, we climbed up the platform at Great Yarmouth railway station with our postman swearing under his breath that it was the longest delivery he had ever done !!

DIARY OF A PUBLICITY GURU

The East Anglia Postbuses.

Carnivals were also the main bread and butter of PR in the '70s, beginning in May and ending in September. A picture of this float – featuring the call girls (telephonists) and street walkers (postmen) – appeared in the window of a local sex shop for some months saying … "We supply the street walkers and call-girls of etc."

But it wasn't all fun and games – lots of work ending up on a flooded display site

DIARY OF A PUBLICITY GURU

But at least the 'bug' was popular - Yes Stamp Bug !!! More about the bug shortly.

Didcot and line-side equipment for collecting mail bags at speed.

Another great PR prop, use of TPOs – travelling post offices where mail is sorted at speed and mail bags picked up en-route from trackside apparatus. This was the romance of the mails, high jinx of speed and sorting through the night with a team of postmen and a million stories.

At Bletchley Railway Station, someone had left a number of milk churns on the 'down' platform edge. A sorter, recently joined and new to the train, looked out of the window for a geographical marker to put out the net – somewhat earlier than usual (before, rather than after, Bletchley Railway Station) – then there was a huge bang – and the whole carriage became bathed in milk. A day later it was a similar problem ... a large bakery produced boxes and boxes and boxes of Swiss rolls that were always taken to London on a parcels train. Delayed somewhat up north, the TPO at speed put out the net, again too early, on the 'Up' and the carriage was filled with hundreds and hundreds of Swiss rolls.

Stamp Bug.

Aside from postcode promotion came Special Stamp Issues and, to promote them, along came Stamp Bug. This cartoon character was introduced, aimed at children, to get them into the habit of collecting all the new issues of stamps – almost a new issue every month. Alongside Stamp Bug came promotional items such as stickers, balloons and – believe it or not – mugs. Alas! – within the post office they became known as 'Bugger Mugs', so the promotional item was dropped.

DIARY OF A PUBLICITY GURU

Television detector van

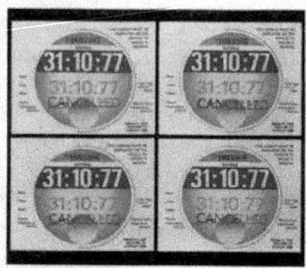

months.
This man is renewing his car licence at the local post office:

Motor vehicle licences

I expect that you will have seen licences like this many times before. Every motor vehicle on the road must have one.
Although first licences can only be issued by the Driver and Vehicle Licensing Centre, Swansea, it is possible to renew a motor vehicle licence at the larger post offices. As you can see from the illustration, licences run for periods of four months or twelve

20

Oh, the days of TV detector vans – what a scary prospect!

Interface with the public – we were asked many times to promote TV License's and we certainly did that. TV Detector Vans would travel around the country from town to town and media jumped on the idea of a threatening story of sensationalism.

But did TV detector vans work? The Regional and Area Managers of TV detection would, on interview, tell the story of how the detector vans kit would recognize the TV station being watched in a house; there were even mobile detector kits for use in flats and high-rise buildings. However, if the truth be told, only on one occasion in the long history of detector vans had the kit been used and proved in court that someone was watching television unlicensed.

Media and PR can have imaginative opportunities – we even came up with the story that detector frogman were out patrolling houseboats on the Norfolk Broads.

The 'Stan the Tramp' campaign went down well in print media –

DIARY OF A PUBLICITY GURU

"Lice yes got plenty of those," said Stan the tramp, "but a license – err well eh no I don't have one of those............"

The papers didn't like it – they felt it crucified the lower class – they all published the picture/caption/story but with a strong anti editorial. Good publicity well publicity but you can't win 'em all !

A character we found near Chelmsford was a foreign gentlemen called Valentine Card – he was extremely photogenic, elderly, but good value pre 14th February celebrations to promote the sending of love !

DIARY OF A PUBLICITY GURU

● Eight Norwich postmen in the overgrown mail bag.

They've got it in the bag!

IT'S the biggest blooming mailbag in the world — unless you know of one bigger!

The giant sack arrived at Norwich parcels sorting office in the overnight articulated lorry from Peterborough, where it was spotted by postman Chris Garrett.

To see just how big it was he and and seven other postmen climbed into it, and found there was still room for a few small packets.

Spirit

The bag, said Mr Garrett, is at least four times the size of a conventional parcels sack, and to add to the "Christmas" spirit the Norwich parcels staff filled it with one postman's packets, which would normally have taken five or six more conventional sacks.

"There's no way any one man could lift it when it's full," said Mr Garrett.

All bagged up with nowhere to go are eight Norwich postmen, Mr Garrett, Mr Chris Baker, Mr Ernie Clapham, Mr Melvin May, Mr Keith Henry, Mr Nigel Blake, Mr Neil Westgate and Mr Bob Russell.

The only thing that worries the Norwich postmen now is that in some other sorting office in the land, nine smaller postmen will one day break their record!

There was even the issue of the sack! Going big was a huge thing in the 70s. Big was beautiful in the '80s – and media went mad on unusual sizes. Here at Norwich Sorting Office, they found the biggest mailbag in the world – unless you know better – so what a shot to get 8 posties in the bag!

So, the 1970s came to an end – a roller coaster ride of Postcodes, Stamp Promotions, Marketing and media services – alongside County Shows and of course some glamour!

Chapter 5
Animals History & the Blue Dot Experience

From the 1980s – Attacks on Posties promotion.

POSTMAN - DOG BITES

CASE No. 2

TONTO THE TERROR
(TERRIER)

CASE No. 5

MAJOR – THE ONE IN CHARGE

The world of self-adhesive letters was new to public relations and displays suffered somewhat!

DIARY OF A PUBLICITY GURU

Displays portraying the Post Office's history continued to be a strong theme but, in the world of Coach to Code, not all went well! Maybe it was the start of EEC fishing regs !

Dick Chipperfield of Chipperfield's Circus at Winter Farm – the winter quarters of the travelling tented circus in the training barn!

And the '80s highlighted the anti of 'never work with animals or children'. Here in the circus – yes, the TV detector vans were back just checking on the lion tamer watching TV with his star lions! Made some great print media coverage

Hygiene in the sorting office was paramount – all those bags stored in warm rooms attracted vermin, so most sorting offices employed the post office cat to keep away mice and rats. A wide number of sorting office cats became media stars in their areas.

The '80s glorified these PR elements like this Victorian Pillar Box in Brunswick green and old gold, set up here near St Johns Abbey Gateway in Colchester – someone came along and posted a letter thinking it was an in-use service box.
There was the old……………….and the new!

And in the 80s older post-boxes became collectors items – some post office yards became graveyards for old boxes – some were bought up and used as private posting boxes – some went abroad !!

DIARY OF A PUBLICITY GURU

Seasonal activities of weather and Christmas always gathered good media reaction. Above: In deepest Norfolk, it's deep and crisp for mail deliveries. Below: A British Air Ferries 'flying postie' Santa Flight

The 1980s shows continued to be a major part of the PR scene and, when blue dots started to appear on envelopes, questions started to be asked about their significance … so the Blue Dot Experience was born.

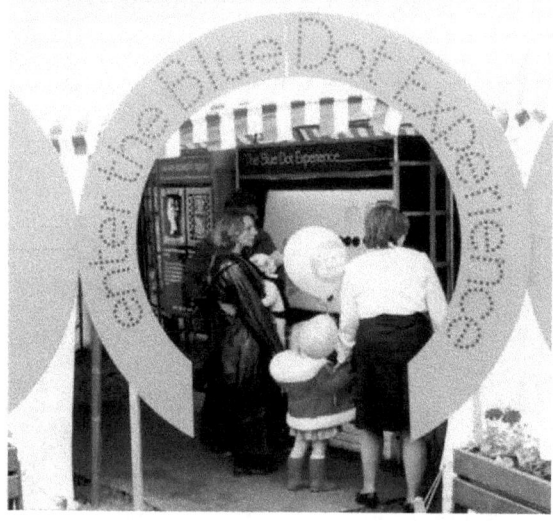

County Show time in the 1980s - Notice the details – Show Hostesses dressed almost as airline girls (copied from British Air Ferries) – with blue dot scarves and the customary Post Office stickers that everyone wanted – indeed, on day one of a county show, they ran out of stickers and had to get more printed overnight!

DIARY OF A PUBLICITY GURU

PR exhibits continued with the theme of postcodes and blue dots – all the while educating the nation. Machines to sort the mail would be the future of the Royal Mail, developing from blue dot recognition to OCR – optical character recognition. In fact, PR for postcode usage went from strength to strength and an organization called 'Lighter than Air' gained great response to flying hot air balloons both for customers and competition winners, as well as just pure advertising.

Indeed, a little plane trailing a 'Use the Postcode' banner flew perilously close to the Wimbledon Tennis Courts on the same day the then Chairman of the Post Office attended the finals. So close did the plane fly to the courts that it interfered with the game, distracted the players and, in fact, stopped play. This was much to the disgust of the Post Office Chairman, who rang the PR Publicity HQ to demand the plane be shot down!

DIARY OF A PUBLICITY GURU

The 'Blue-Dot tie and engineers rig the exhibition tent !

DIARY OF A PUBLICITY GURU

Alongside the shows and the Blue Dot Experience, seaside postcard promotions were a key to marketing greater volumes of post. Attractive girls made promo appearances around the country, making photo calls from beach to beach.

Unfortunately, the 'Post a Little Happiness' tee-shirts were problematic in that, by holding giant postcards they could cut out the Hap and read, "Post a little piness (penis!)"

Chapter 6
Poco Balloon Races and the Golden Hinde

The Blue Dot Experience needed publicity to draw the crowds and a giant Poco elephant head was gas-filled and flown from the marquee.

During a Young Farmers day at the Essex Show, some tipsy YF's thought it might be a great idea to cut free the giant floating head.

It's 00.50am and a call from the Air Ministry: "Are you in charge of the Post Office, as we have had several reports from aircraft pilots that a giant elephant's head with the word *Post Office* on it has been seen floating around in the sky? In fact, it is a danger to aircraft on final approach to Stansted Airport – what are you going to do about it?"

Alas, at that time of night, it is difficult to know what to say or do.

So, a call to PEB Imports and Space Age Promotions cleared the air, so to speak. The gas they used would gradually abate as the air cooled, so eventually the Poco head would decrease in size as the gas changed in make-up.

The air ministry took this info with a pinch of salt!

Poco flying high above the Essex County Show Ground.

DIARY OF A PUBLICITY GURU

At the same show, the international Poco Balloon Race was on offer to the show visitors – simply fill in a coupon with your address, complete with postcode – attach to a balloon and launch.

The reply address for people finding the balloon was the office and, over the following weeks, many balloon labels were returned – the one that travelled the furthest would win the prize.

Some labels were returned from nearby Harlow, others from Sawbridgeworth and Suffolk areas. It looked like the prize-winner had a balloon label which had been returned by a fisherman fishing near the sea area 'Dogger Bank' – but then, in the next post, a label returned from New Zealand!

So a call to Met Office 3B enquires for the way of the wind, it's strength and force and indeed the upper air velocity reported that it would be impossible for a 10-inch diameter balloon to travel that far – but, if your Dad is an airline pilot, it is possible to send back a balloon label from afar!

And what's that new space vehicle in the left hand corner I hear you say ?

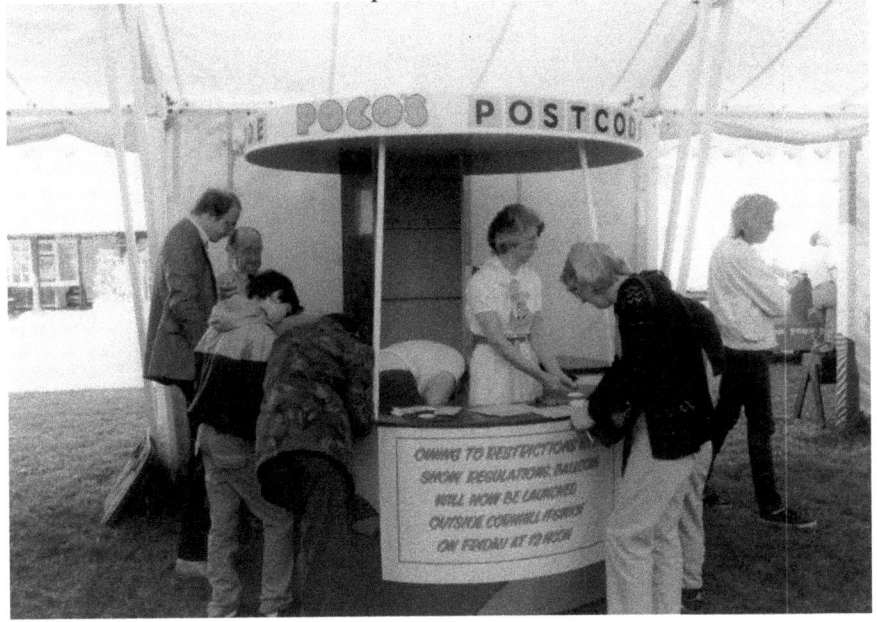

It's the new ride of the year – POCO's Postcode Rocket giving free rides to those who know and use their postcodes in their home address!

The eras of the '70s and '80s were really the end of the gin and tonic man – the person I worked for was previously a salesman in post office telephones and saw a job advertised as a new public relations officer – so he read a book called teach yourself PR and was the first of these gin and tonic men! Dear Johnnie Johnson how he taught the basics of public relations hic hic hic!

Christmas in the late 1980s finished with a new ride - Santa and his reindeer!

Indeed, postcode promotions went to the ends of the earth to get public interest and coverage – the boathouse at Oxford for the University boat race crew fortunately had its own postcode and, shortly before the race weekend, posters went up in the OX postcode areas to encourage use of postcodes – with local staff instructed to remove posters at short notice if Oxford did not win … fortunately they did!

DIARY OF A PUBLICITY GURU

The '80s were the time of 'best' events – Best Postie – TVAM ran a Competition to find the best postman or postwoman and I well remember interviewing a Mrs McKenzie who lived in a sort of castle building in deepest Suffolk.

She had nominated her postie – and, on arrival at her home around 11.30am, I found her still in her dressing gown on the phone complaining to the Jimmy Young Radio 2 programme about some national issue. She asked her maid to make me a cuppa which tasted revolting as it was a lapsang brew – probably made in a cigarette ashtray! However, a few weeks later, she was to go to the TVAM studios in London; I picked her up and took her to Diss railway station to get the London train very early in the morning.

"I don't eat breakfast" said Mrs Mc – but, in the restaurant car when smoked kippers went past, she changed her mind and said she would! Unfortunately, the first bite had a fish bone on the fork and Mrs Mc swallowed it, getting it stuck in her throat and, for the rest of the day, she coughed and spluttered … even being interviewed in the studio, the coughing continued.

However, more popular were the Best Post Office competitions, both in print media and on BBC local radio stations, giving ample opportunities for all sorts of coverage including the final presentations.

This was also the time of international pr in that the government department of the DTI were promoting Great Britain across the world. I was asked to look after a Canadian tv crew and the DTI ambassador girl – they were doing a piece on the British Post Office, the system the works, and wanted location shots of the post office mechanization workshop at Martlesham near Ipswich. The crew went off and I followed their vehicle with the DTI girl.

"They all ask for it you know," she said, the Arab tv crews are the worst – we give them hospitality at the Tower of London restaurant, then they ask for it!"

"So how do you react?" said I. "Well I just said love to be with you but what about your wife. "And if they are no married," I said.

"Well great super, love to go to bed with you," she said, "but I'd lose my job."

On that note the tv crew finished filming………………

Away from media activities - another great publicity idea was Lorry Driver of the Year competitions, in which Royal Mail Drivers always did well – so, above, Anglia Television news do a piece at the Post Office marquee.

DIARY OF A PUBLICITY GURU

Lorry Driver of the year show was normally at Cranfield and very close was RAF Chicksands. I think after viewing the post office stand on year they were keen for a post office display at their open day. I was invited to the base and introduced to a giant American guy- the base boss, the General. With a very firm handshake he said," Do you know what we do here – we listen to the reds." He then took a drag on a giant cigar before turning to his tiny officer assistant and saying, "That's what we do isn't Abner." He said,"yes sir," the General then turned back to me and said, "But we don't talk about it do we Abner," And Abner retorted, "No sir we don't." An American experience of a lifetime.......

With the Post Office and mail movement, there was always an opportunity for doing something different. Here a regular rail service moved bulk mail, from a financial handling unit up country, to Crewe on a twice a week basis. This was the post office SuperTrain – but from time to time it broke down and mail was transferred to air-flights and the flying postie.

In the '80s, Poco went from strength to strength – seen here at Whipsnade Zoo, near Luton, with his pals!

The '80s were also an 'any excuse for glamour' era – and Datapost Pilots were always keen for a press pic with a glamorous PR assistant, no matter what time of day or night.

DIARY OF A PUBLICITY GURU

Philately was an '80s thing as well and Stamp Bug came into his own with the Stamp Buggy and lots of freebies.

DIARY OF A PUBLICITY GURU

Well Buggar me!

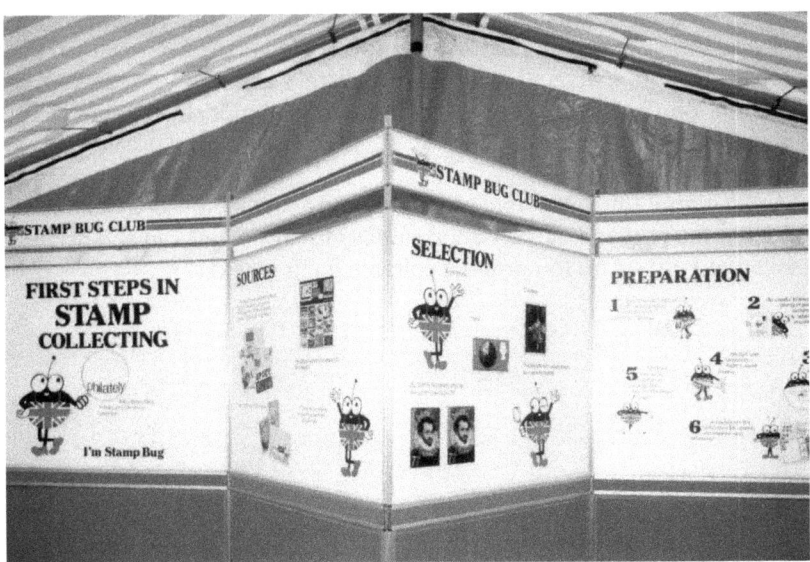

DIARY OF A PUBLICITY GURU

The Picture Postcard Voyage of the Golden Hinde was an event to promote the sending of postcards whilst on holiday. The Golden Hinde sailed around the coastline of the British Isles where major Post Office PR events were planned at different ports, welcoming local mayors and dignitaries aboard. However, it didn't all go to plan. At each location, Post Office champagne flowed freely – and even the captain and crew enjoyed the booze. So much so, that the good folk at Brighton were all ready to receive this splendid vessel – yes, here it comes – but, oh dear, there it goes! In a drunken stupor, the captain forgot to dock at the location.

At Great Yarmouth there were more problems – no gangway available to link the vessel to the port and, at very short notice, a Royal Mail van and driver were dispatched to Felixstowe to borrow a suitable gang plank!

Welcome aboard everyone – you can get your all into a letter or postcard!

This was a good idea …. and it was mine! Postcode your valuables, postcode your pushbike. After all, a postcode is unique to your address with the number or name of the house. Police loved it – and so did John Craven's Newsround, who did the national PR launch in Bedford.

Excuses for celebrations were '80s style and big ones, giant cakes and PR 'jollies' became the norm …

Chapter 7
Postman Pat and other Personalities

A long came Postman Pat ... Ivor Wood of Woodland Animation asked us to the BBC Launch in London – and the Post Office and Postman Pat became synonymous! New ride machine for the shows!

Cashing in on Postman Pat! Yes the van in the carnival float did travel around the trailer and along with the music was a big winner!

DIARY OF A PUBLICITY GURU

The days of the Postman Pat Disco, Colouring Competitions and giveaways!

DIARY OF A PUBLICITY GURU

Above: The '80s were personality times – famous guitarist, the late Bert Weedon, judged the children's letter-writing competition.

Below: Radio One DJ Mike Read becomes a postman for the morning round – and, to get the publicity, we get him to swear in live on-air – to be a good postman, deliver all the mail, and promise to always use the postcode!

DIARY OF A PUBLICITY GURU

Above: The late Dr David Bellamy appears at a marketing event after we presented a package of sending all things through the post, including plants and trees!
It was Dutch elm disease year and he promoted Elms Across Europe to replace diseased trees.

Personalities always worked well, as did Mother's Day Sunday Delivery (above) of flowers from postmen in Kings Lynn.

Chapter 8
Crime & Stamps & Transport

Then there was the next era of Cop-a-Card from a copper!

Yes... many, many large sized cards were printed and distributed to, firstly, Hertfordshire Constabulary. The idea was to let coppers on the beat have a number of cards to be collected by Children and get them streetwise in the name of the law, getting to know their local bobby. The launch was done at the Herts Constabulary HQ at Welwyn Garden City, with a great spread of buffet and wine for the press. I was told in no uncertain terms that, if I was stopped and breathalyzed on the way home, just say I had been drinking with the Chief Constable! The scheme was a great success for postcode promotion and for the police to stamp out crime.

Stamp Issues were a good excuse to do something different – the Greenwich Meridian Stamp issue gave the opportunity to fly along the meridian line from the Greenwich Observatory to schools, villages and communities actually on the meridian. The helicopter, complete with BBC TV news crew, popped in and made the final destination – Swavesey, near Cambridge – where everyone came out to see the landing. To celebrate the stamp issue, we got the local pub to create the Meridian Cocktail – a lovely golden concoction that could leave a warm glow in the body. Wonder if it's still available now?

DIARY OF A PUBLICITY GURU

Above: BBC TV cameraman, the late Hank Hankin, unloads his camera from the Greenwich Meridian Helicopter – the TV crew had travelled with us from the Greenwich Observatory in London.

Left: Landing in Swavesey, near Cambridge. Following re-fuelling, some joy rides were given to locals to view the meridian line from above.

Left: With flying still in mind, I was permitted to take over controls on a British Air Ferries Viscount after taking journalists to see the mail being delivered to Jersey in the Channel Islands.
Great day, breakfast over the channel, sorting office, etc ... plus duty frees and back in the office before lunch!

Then came the letter-writing train – this was a pen-shaped train with a giant nib on the front. 1000s of school children were en-route to see it at Norwich, but the railway people had put it away from the station on a freight siding. Once I mentioned about the buses and coaches of children en-route, it was moved in double quick time to a platform.

Above: Creating life-size fibre-glass horses for the Mail Coach Stamp Issue was a bit of a feat. However, the float went down well – with many people believing, they were real horses.

Below: Poco continued to be popular – we even did a small pack for village fetes and charities with stickers and prizes to promote Postcodes.

The '80s continued with Post Office Marketing in a big way – potential customers were flown to Rotterdam to wait for the inaugural Datapost flight from Luton. But all did not go as planned. There was to be a meal at the airport before the flight arrived – Dutch Post Office colleague, Peter Optenburgh, introduced himself and welcomed everyone to Rotterdam before asking me to say pre-meal grace – in Dutch. Alas, I only speak two languages – English and Filthy. But, to my fortune over my shoulder, the Datapost flight arrived one hour early – so, after explaining I had always wanted to be a part-time English vicar and that I did not speak Dutch, I talked adlib about the flight. The return passenger flight to Luton was also problematic – on descent to Luton airport we were parallel to the runway rather than lined up to the runway, so we had to go around again. The pilot was a first timer at Luton.

This was 1984 and there were numerous stamp issues, all warranting a launch – even at a Cattle Market in Tring ... oh, the things we did for the PO!

Chapter 9
Poco's Postbus and Concorde

1984 and the era of the promotion buses taking postcodes and letter-writing on the road.

Welcome aboard *Poco's Postbus* – in reception check out your postcode for your address on the new computerized PAF File.
Just look at the state-of-the-art computer back in the day!

Lots to see downstairs in the postcode exhibition area ...but, upstairs ...

A video cinema, galley and VIP lounge.

Yes ... food and drink served to VIP guests. Alas, in the early days, eating from an aircraft type meal tray could be difficult as visitors boarding the exhibition area downstairs would make the bus sway – many councilors and mayors had stained ties as the fork slipped – but the answer was stabilizers, one fitted at each corner of the bus, electronically wound down to correct the vehicle.

But, where did the bus come from, you may ask? Ensign Bus at Purfleet in east London – they specialised in tour buses and hop-on/hop-off vehicles for the capital and major towns and cities all over the world. MD Peter Newman was so very helpful with the *Poco Bus* fitted out by the Post Office Engineering Depot in Bamber Bridge. The bus went everywhere –schools, trade exhibitions and county shows,

Poco's Postbus galley at the top of the central stairway where much booze was served!

DIARY OF A PUBLICITY GURU

It's 1984 and a competition brainwave occurred – Concorde flies at the same speed that it takes optical recognition sorting machines to recognize postcodes on letters – so why not use the PR Opportunities Budget to get underway a special competition to have a supersonic trip on Concorde?

But, alas, Concorde normally only flies from Heathrow and it's expensive for take-off and landing.

Therefore, why not bring it to Stansted where:
1.) less expensive on the ground
2.) quieter airport, and
3.) more media bets.

But, to get Concorde to Stansted in 1986, fuel costs £800 each way so why not sell subsonic seats, with a coach back and forth from Stansted each way, to get the money back and offer a subsonic ride on the famous aircraft? What a great idea!

The competition winner and guests arrived to a champagne reception with loads of media. Once on board the pilot says: "On take-off, we'll be turning left" … 3 minutes later, he corrects it to say turning right … he still thought he was at Heathrow, or that's what he said!

DIARY OF A PUBLICITY GURU

On the flight deck and with prize winners aboard.

Christmas presents from the real Santa on arrival back on firm ground.

A week later ... who opened Luton's new Post Office in the Arndale Centre?

Well, Lorraine Chase, of course ...

it was right near the airport!

Chapter 10
The Glitz of the VSOE

Stamp launches and 'jollies' ... well, why not? The late Terrence Cuneo, a brilliant designer, for the Famous Trains Stamp Issue ... why not charter the British Pullman Carriages of the Venice Simplon Orient Express and invite guests? The train took 178 passengers ... yes, invite them: "Would you like a trip on the British Pullman Carriages?" ... "What, Venice?" said the guest ... "No, Didcot Steam Sidings out of London Paddington. But you do get to meet Sally Thomsett, famous actress from the Railway Children!"

Stamp Designer Terrance Cuneo always hid a little mouse in all his artwork – when I visited him at his studio in a gorgeous barn in Surrey, he showed us his work, including some great paintings for the army. He said there was one painting where, as usual, he had hidden the mouse ... but – alas! – after many hours study, I still couldn't find it!

DIARY OF A PUBLICITY GURU

All aboard th

COLCHESTER-based Paul Diggens, left, is head of the Post Office Eastern Region public-relations team. He chartered the British carriages of the Orient Express to publicise the newest stamp issue of famous trains on an unfamiliar route through eastern region territory, with a film star aboard. DEREK DREW went along for the ride. . . .

PHILATELY, some say, gets you nowhere.
The Post Office doesn't agree — it makes around £6 million from it to add to this year's projected £80 million profit.
And pre-sale orders from collectors for the newest issue funded the exotic launch of five famous trains stamps on the most famous train of them all. The Venice Simplon-Orient Express went west — occidentally, of course — with 200 postal officials, enthusiasts and their guests.
Hauled by the Great Wes-

When we did the recci on the Venice Simplon Orient Express in august of the year before the charter we happened to meet the late singer Perry Como who was recording his Christmas Show on the train. Decked with holly and ivy and other festive trimmings it was difficult to get your head around the fact that it was a 75F summer day.

Perry Como was accompanied by some big heavy-weight minders – I will always remember one of them in a loud gruff voice saying, "who's got Como's ticket!"

DIARY OF A PUBLICITY GURU

Sip Post Office/VSOE Champagne with the Police Band to play us away!

Below: Some great VSOE hospitality with a VIP.

Below: A real TPO – Travelling Post Office mail exchange at speed, just like it was done in the good old days!

Bands and presentations at every station.

DIARY OF A PUBLICITY GURU

Then there was the Safety at Sea Stamp Issue and what better way to launch a stamp than again charter the VSOE Pullman carriages out of London Liverpool Street and take guests to Cromer? Until the end of the 1950s, the railways moved lifeboats free of charge around the country, so why not have a flat wagon on the rear of the train and donate an inshore lifeboat to Cromer? So, with a great deal of planning and displays and brass bands at every station, another 'jolly' with Sally Thomsett aboard.

At Cromer, the lifeboat would be taken through the streets and the lifeboat would be launched from the end of the pier, then an air-sea helicopter would rescue the commemorative covers and stamps before the presentation on the stage at the end of the pier theatre.

BBC radio presenter and journalist of the Radio 4 *Today* programme the late John Timpson was in Cromer, his home-town, making a programme. He was not impressed with the razzmatazz of the Post Office arriving in town, saying publicly that this did not do much for Cromer!

We were only giving the town an inshore lifeboat to save lives – must have been an off day for him!

DIARY OF A PUBLICITY GURU

 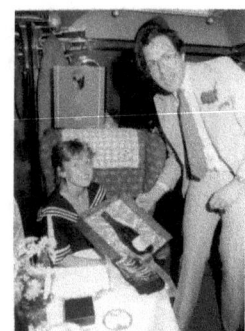

Above: Being interviewed by BBC Radio Norfolk on the journey from Norwich to Cromer, and presentation of VSOE champagne to a competition winner enjoying the journey.

Below: BBC journalist John Timpson complaining about the Post Office day in Cromer – he didn't get a ride on the VSOE or on stage at the end of the pier theatre!

Above: Everyone turns out in Cromer to greet the new in-shore lifeboat – a horse-drawn vehicle from the station to the pier and people put their hands through the top windows of the Pullman Carriages at the station asking for commemorative VSOE memorabilia.

Chapter 11
Diversifications

A stamp of glass – or rather a glass stamp – this was unveiled and presented to Willis Faber Dumas PLC at Ipswich, as their glass building featured on one of the many stamp issues in the 1980s.
Just couldn't get my head around a garden 6 floors up! Presentations to all!

DIARY OF A PUBLICITY GURU

The new look PR team in Ipswich.

Just look at the birthday cake idea – giant cakes coming into fashion as we congratulated the Southend Evening Echo coming of age.

DIARY OF A PUBLICITY GURU

More Cop-a-Cards ... this time at Bedford. Stamp issues every month and even a donation of an ambulance – these were the times of spending the cash.

Above: PR Assistant Millie Haynes appears to be making a vase for the pottery stamp issue & Religious service of blessing an ambulance!

Above: Sir Issac Newton Stamps – so apples for everyone in care homes.

Left: Being held up yet again by a highwayman, with athlete Sharron Davies, for a torch relay race in Luton.

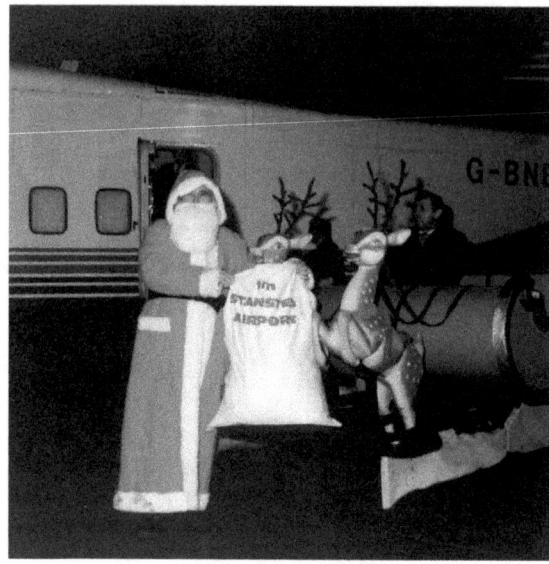

There's always an excuse for an anniversary or occasion – like inventing something – a million letters handled at Stansted Airport with the flying postie – if it's not quite right, who's going to go back and count them all?

Above: Here's TV personality Ruth Madoc, from Hi-de-Hi days, launching the Wishing Well Appeal. Must have been a busy Week – starting to look tired.

DIARY OF A PUBLICITY GURU

Special appearance at Oxford.

Who said never work with animals and children in media and PR? An Australian Stamp Issue warrants a kangaroo from down-under to make a personal appearance to promote the stamps.

But, under the Dangerous Wild Animals Act, you need a special license and permission from the City and County Council.

Clubb-Chipperfield, who owned lots of animals for TV and film appearances, had all the licenses – although the Oxford Mayor rang to complain.

It seems that a year back, a performing elephant from a circus was taken into Oxford City Centre and the elephant did a whoopsie on the front lawn of the City Hall and the Mayor was not too pleased.

"How dare you bring a wild animal to my city?" said the Mayor.

"Let me copy you the license from your local department," I said, "together with Clubb-Chipperfield's license."

The phone line went silent ... then blank.

We mostly get it right!

Just look at BBC Newsreader Jan Leeming – a great day in High Wycombe.

I was first introduced to Zoo Theatre in London back in the mid-1970s. Being told to collect animal costumes from Covent Garden in London, I left early in my car and arrived just when they opened at 9.30am. There, to my amazement, was every animal face and costume you could think of – and very professional too. For years we hired animal costumes for the entire carnival season.

For every stamp issue and launch, there was always an opportunity to dress-up. Here in Norwich, lunch for customers on a barge went to plan, on a very hot day.

TPOs – Travelling Post Office events always took a great deal of planning, especially if it was going to be live TV, before the days of satellite dishes. The trip from Norwich to London was re-timed to Look East schedules with additional postmen brought in to ensure pick-up of letters from different stations at new timings ensuring the mail got through. What the TV briefing did not give was, wear thick socks as it can be very cold on a TPO with the net open for mail pick-up at speed. A very cold TV Director had to have a very big winter warmer at Liverpool Street!

Chapter 12
Promotions to the Forefront

A re-fit of *Poco's Postcode Postbus* and *The Post Office Experience* got underway. The bus was tight and displays needed to be taken back to give better public space as per the *'Write It' Bus*. On wet show days the bus could be full, with guests sheltering from the rain packed in like sardines.

DIARY OF A PUBLICITY GURU

The letter-writing *'Write It' Bus* launched with Anglia TV presenter Paul Barnes and Colchester Town Mayor Bob Russell and daylight fireworks to boot. Just look at the nice carpet on the floor and roof!

Inside the 'Write It' Bus – a far wider exhibition area.

Above: A new publicity prop – bigger and better and well-branded for press pix – the 'Write It' pen.

Below: Poco had a make-over too!

DIARY OF A PUBLICITY GURU

1987 and a new idea for the County Shows – a ghost train ride called *The Post Office Experience*. Three 4-seater cars would take passengers for a 90-second ride in a 40-foot artic trailer – but only if you knew your postcode and had written it, along with your complete address, on your ticket.

Trailer with a fold-down side which became the loading bay. The rails were then connected to the inside of the trailer and the cars would be set up. One at a time they would push through the double spring doors and do a kidney shape journey through animated effects, like a Royal Mail train on a roller belt. A flying postie plane that moved from the ceiling and a selection of stamps that lit up ... and Postman Pat and Jess the cat waving at the end.

But, using a cardboard shoe box, I showed the motor transport division that we could do more with the ghost train ride by having two re-trackable pods to increase the size and ride – and during the winter months this was achieved giving far greater availability for display items and a longer ride.

Two 5kw generators were stuck underneath just in case of no mains power, music was provided along with sound effects throughout the ride, and I applied for a Fairground Operators License to take *The Post Office Experience* all over the country.

This made good use of the new Exhibition Bus – Bus No 2 – the *Write It Bus*. Or, as we referred to it in the office, the right tit bus with the big boob and nipple on the side! But, joking apart, this was a new idea with stairs going to the top deck at the front of the bus and a new set of stairs at the back – displays throughout and carpeted everywhere – very plush!

DIARY OF A PUBLICITY GURU

Great show jackets too!

DIARY OF A PUBLICITY GURU

This was the highlight of the show and many awards were made as the queues got longer and longer for customers to enjoy *The Post Office Experience*.

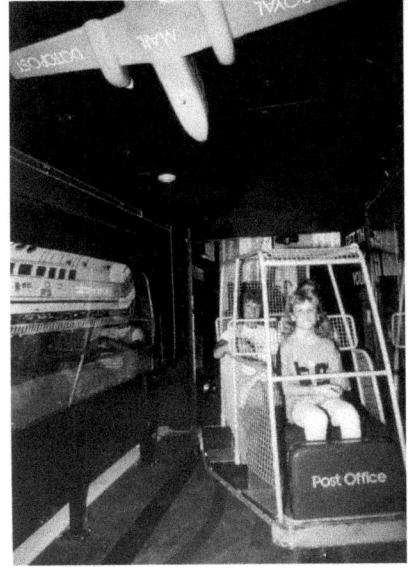

The Post Office Experience – the cars, track and controls came from Modern Products in Grimsby. The right-hand picture (above) shows, behind the late Mick Heath (joint designer of *The Experience*), the booth for writing out your address and postcode on your ticket.

If you didn't know it, you checked it out on the *Postcode Bus* reception.

DIARY OF A PUBLICITY GURU

Postcode ticket to ride.

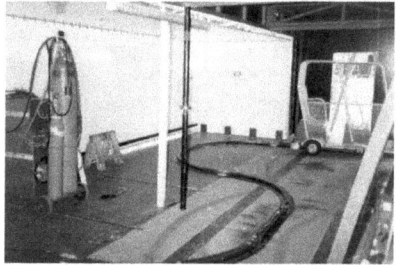
The first track layout.

Checking your postcode

Very rare, but it can happen – a derailment! Post Office engineers on hand to help.

'Write It' Bus, Poco's Postbus, Post Office Experience, Postman Pat rides and a ticket office! Busy show days – especially when a Minister showed up! Yes – Nigel Lawson MP, former Chancellor of the Exchequer, was most impressed with the Post Office Stand.

Two postman drivers became known as 'The Bus Boys' – just how many miles did they take the two exhibition buses and *The Post Office Experience* in the UK?

On the motorway one day, lots of flashing lights – sadly the generator trailer that attached to the buses had a flat-tyre; the rubber and the wheel gradually wore away to the axle. But Alan and Arthur still arrived in time to set up the show. What great Post Office ambassadors!

But, sometimes, in remote delivery locations you had to go to the ends of the earth to meet with TV crews to get the shot!

Chapter 13
Poco's Postcode Song and more Stamps

To begin with, during the '80s, Poco postcode education went from *Poco in the Jungle* to *Poco's Postcode Circus*.

To get the right circus feel we joined Austen Brothers Circus when they were tented up in Ipswich – being shown the ropes by Miss Austen.

This was the time for Poco to release a record and create a fan club. With our contacts in the Postman Pat franchise, the song writer Brian Daley was pleased to compose *The Postcode Song* c/w a 'B' side of *Writing Letters*. So, with song and lyrics agreed, Brian introduced us to Kerry, who was a runner-up singer on *Saturday Superstore* hosted by DJ Mike Read. To the recording studios we go, with my deputy Mick Heath, at the end of Oxford Street in London's West End to meet with Kerry who came from Glasgow.

Then it's out to the record pressing factory in West London for the process to begin – a run of 10,000 records.

So, with music for Poco, what about the prop of *Poco's Postcode Band*, with animation too? In the Poco Fan club we also produced educational comics !

Not a top 10 release but what about some gold records? Competitions in local newspapers and radio stations and press presentations of gold records for doing it – all in the name of postcode promotions, including *McDonalds*!

Then time for the music video promotion film, with showings in key cinemas throughout the UK.

This is the cinema in Oxford – the production was filmed in the recording studios with Kerry and in a top-notch nightclub in Norwich. Poco's fan club went from strength to strength with a dozen comics produced and a dedicated phone-line to listen to his record.

Time to get back to Philately – and Ely Cathedral is featured on one of the special stamp issues. To launch the stamp a mail coach run from Cambridge with the Bishop of Ely aboard. Very red nose … must have been on the communion wine early in the day. Through the autumn mists we travelled before an unveiling ceremony in the cathedral for these Christmas Stamps.

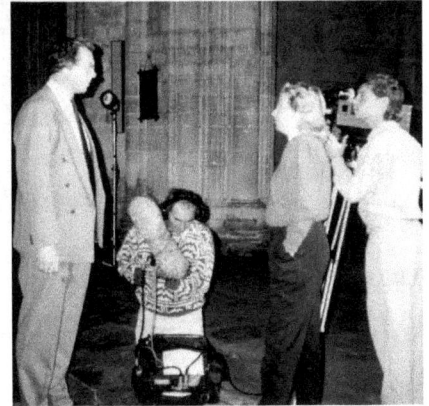

As we had the stamp designer with us, it was time for a TV interview, but alas these were the days of the syco ties – colourful and not really in keeping with religion. Fortunately, the verger said I could borrow his tie, but he was off home at 6.00pm so needed it back before then!

And, so, the stamp unveiling – the stamp in a stained-glass window for the Ely Cathedral Museum collection.

The '80s – an era of threat-based management. We are out to get you said the establishment – particularly TV licensing – and *Detector Man* was born.

Even got the 'OK' from the TV campaigner the late Mary Whitehouse, just checking your TV licence, ma'am!

Another promotion meeting up with singing personality Frankie Vaughan. One good thing about the Post Office – we knew everyone's address.

DIARY OF A PUBLICITY GURU

New Post Office building openings would always be done with a touch of glamour and panache. Here TV personality, the late broadcaster Anne Gregg, is joined by the Military to fanfare the official opening.

The always useful portable curtains – track and cord ever-present on an exhibition display unit and Velcro for the plaque.

The official opening stamp and afterwards a super Pullman train journey for VIPs with a TPO sorting carriage on the back to boot.

Life on the road – sometimes need to stop off in a layby for a cuppa – some moans from a certain BBC regional TV presenter – was delayed along the A140 on the way back to Norwich as I was following your buses in a convoy! Well good publicity then.

DIARY OF A PUBLICITY GURU

Postman Pat-a-gram was a great idea with a van all spruced up and stickers and gifts for whoever's birthday it was and the van, Postman Pat and Jess the cat would make a personal appearance.

Late '80s and the style of the presentation and celebration cakes began – big is beautiful, big is best – gets the message and branding over in the icing.

Sadly, as the 1980's came to an end, so did the TPO's – travelling post office journeys on the rails were consigned to history with TPO carriages being sent to preservation railway societies or scrapped.

Left: This was one of the last journeys into London Liverpool Street.

Chapter 14
Canal Post Office and Gallantry Stamps

So, how were the 1990s in PR?

Industrial Archaeology Stamps gave every opportunity to do something with the canals – and hospitality too …

How about a floating post office? Yes … a post office on a canal narrowboat selling stamps and commemorative covers.

DIARY OF A PUBLICITY GURU

Then we had Gallantry Stamps – a great excuse to take war veterans and competition winners to the battlefields of France. Final checks aboard the aircraft at Southend, before guests arrive and we fly to Caen.

The welcome to Southend Airport and the march to the plane would have the music from a military band. Driving along the M25 in 1990, the phone went – "Chief Inspector McKay here – I'm putting the dogs in at 6.00am."

"Dogs," I said, "What dogs?"

"You have a Military Band at Southend Airport tomorrow, normal security checking it out," said the voice.

"Oh yes," I said, "thank you, Inspector."

"It's Chief Inspector, and I know what you are doing and where you are – you are currently on the M25 near Potters Bar," said the voice.

"I certainly am," I said, "and many thanks for your help, Chief Inspector."

And the dogs did go in early, Southend Airport Security told us.

What a day! A Sergeant Major barked orders and marched the veterans across the airport apron to the waiting plane, with TV crews in attendance, stamps to the forefront.

Above: The Battlefields of France.

At the Bayeux Cemetery, a very special ceremony of the laying of a wreath. I had to go to British Legion HQ in London to buy one in the spring – they are not usually available until Remembrance Day in November and I kept it in my briefcase, explaining to customs in Southend what I was doing with a real live poppy wreath – not a drug mule.

In France the PR staff set themselves up in a French café for a little rest! A very successful PR day with the pilot of British Air Ferries flying along the French D-Day landing coastline for all to see on the way back.

Chapter 15
New Look to Christmas

Having a Walt Disney style brain, we were given the task of a *Post Early for Christmas* campaign early in the summer. So, after the success of *The Post Office Experience*, the ghost train ride, what about a sleigh ride to the real Santa's Grotto. From green grass through snow all in the back of a 40-foot artic trailer. So ... the project commenced.

Once again Modern Products, the ghost train ride specialists, were involved. Instead of just forward motion, once children alighted in Santa's Grotto, we needed to send the empty sleigh back for more visitors. A different control mechanism Modern Products had not come across before, but they rose to the challenge. Fitting out of the *Santa 'Grotty' Grotto* was done at the Post Office Motor Transport Depot at Kidbrooke, south east London, where it was rigorously tested for safety.

DIARY OF A PUBLICITY GURU

The final touch was snow laid deep and crisp and even over chicken wire it was so realistic !

Snowman and reindeer moved and the snow finished after the final archway.

Yes, a magical journey and a singing choir too.

A present and sticker for everyone and, behind the scenes, speed required to keep up with demand. In the 7-week run-up to Christmas, Santa saw over 10,000 children. On one occasion he was dozing as there are only so many times you can say hello, what's your name, what would you like for Christmas? But media liked it – acres of coverage and hours of broadcast footage.

Someone who became a great friend and colleague was *Sky at Night*'s Patrick Moore and, whenever there was a 'Space' stamp, we would ask Patrick to make a special PR appearance. Patrick was a key ingredient at several Astronomy or Haley's Comet Stamp Issues. So much so, media would fight to attend the event once it was on the grapevine.

For Haley's Comet, Patrick had agreed to make a presentation using 35 mm slides. We had to fax him all the details to his West Sussex home – in those days, computer messages were few and far between. However, fax machines were key to transmitting messages – and three times we faxed Patrick only to be told he had not received anything. A final phone call to him – and he checked his fax machine … "No wonder nothing has come through" he said, 'the cat's bottom is sitting on the receive button."

Arriving in Cambridge, Patrick told me he had forgotten to bring his slides from home and explained he was sorry he was delayed, but he had called into the Planetarium in London. He said to the girl in the shop, "My name is Patrick Moore and I want to buy every slide you have on Haley's Comet." To which the girl said, "We know who you are – you are the patron of this organization and you can have anything in the shop free of charge." 6 slides and Patrick's dialogue kept everyone amused for 50 – yes, 50 – minutes! What a presenter!

Chapter 16
The National Lottery and the Post Office

The 1990s saw the launch of the *National Lottery* and the Post Office wanted a great part of the action as a national retailer and its need for new business – government in that era were taking away business and hoping everyone would buy TV Licences and Road Fund Licences (aka Car Tax), etc, on-line.

So, there was a purge of media activity – giant fingers, mini-skirted females and a wide variety of dressing up for the occasion. The lottery organization was Camelot – so why not use the name? Although it's never wise to get involved with animals or children in media events – things can go so, so wrong – how about a camel with a lot of lottery tickets on its humps? ... Camelot!

Events would be staged at both Oxford and Cambridge in one day – and, under the Dangerous Wild Animal Act, we had had wild animals in those locations before.

Hidden away in the car park under the archway of St. Aldates Post Office in Oxford – Clubb-Chipperfield brought their camel and it took only a few minutes to dress and get a rider. It was then brought into the Post Office entrance – much to the amazement of the public and media – to a fanfare entrance – and it all went well.

Lottery launch – with camel and all for Camelot! The camel seemed to be very used to members of the public and I believe it had been in Chipperfield's Circus act.

All went well during the morning launch in Oxford, but the Cambridge afternoon launch ... well, that was a different story!

Cambridge's Post Office in the City Centre had a service road behind it, so it was easy to park up and get the camel positioned for the media at the entrance to the post office.

With most media shots, the local paper wanted an inside pic – so camel and attendant were walked to the front counter.

Unfortunately, the counter clerk had some very strong after-shave that the camel took offence to and it started making strange noises and spitting out towards customers. A hasty dive to its horse – sorry, camel-box and van at the rear had to be made at speed.

DIARY OF A PUBLICITY GURU

But celebrations of promotions of the lottery went amok!

A follow-up Lottery event took place at Cambridge once the scratch cards were launched.

The late Lois Maxwell, the original Miss Moneypenny from *007 Film* days, arrived for an overnighter before an early press call at the post office.

Entertaining her at dinner, she spoke about the films and Sean Connery and the many stars she had worked with on screen – a very charming and interesting conversation with this delightful actress.

At the crack of dawn, following breakfast, PR Assistant Millie painted one of her finger-nails gold for the press picture with the giant scratch-card – a press launch that went down very well indeed.

Chapter 17
Animals Again

In the continuing quest for new business – Bill Payments were to be promoted by the Post Office and, with the role of animals making good media coverage, another deal was sorted for Clubb-Chipperfield … this time after hours at Banbury Post Office.

This was to highlight the payment of Water Bills and the pelican enjoyed every moment of his star role, pecking everything he could find – including his trainer's fingers! Yes, blood on the carpet too.

The picture went viral and the photographer, Lionel Gretch, used it as his main promotional picture for his business for a number of years until his retirement. The shoot took around 40 minutes.

DIARY OF A PUBLICITY GURU

Yes, the Post Office went to the ends of the earth to find any new business and even wanted publicity for selling cat advent calendars.

Seen here using a real cockerel to launch Cockfield's new Post Office – well, whoever said never work with animals?

DIARY OF A PUBLICITY GURU

Dressing up continued to be a media success – with a famous CS Lewis stamp issue – how about *The Lion, the Witch and the Wardrobe*? Yes, the Oxford City Postmaster dons a wardrobe with a stamp on his nose. The Snow Queen is there too ... unfortunately the crown was so very heavy that the publicity assistant, Millie, had a stiff neck for weeks afterwards.

But then real animals make the picture if you are calm and patient – here a squirrel saves his nuts as a link to a saving scheme!

With a Christmas opening – how about real reindeer? In those days, the Cairngorm Reindeer Centre was the only farm with travelling reindeer – and, on the morning in question, there was a phone call saying their lorry had broken down and they were 50 miles away – just another PR disaster looming.

But, with a little help from contacts in the AA – remember they repaired a wheel on our walking elephant some years back – all's well that ends well.

Yes, animals can be fun in PR and promotions – this Canadian Mountie at Norwich helped launch Bureau de Change on National Canada Day.

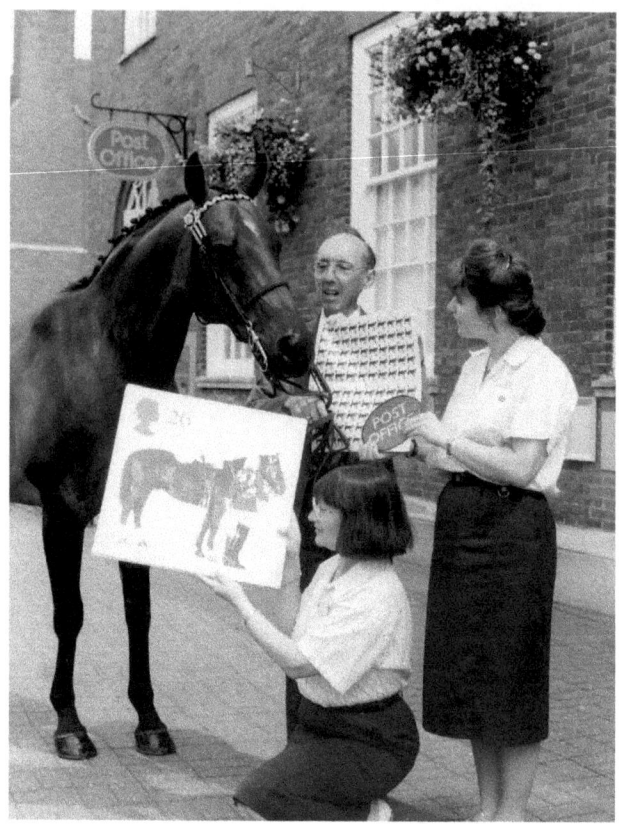

Nice hooves! Yes, horses make good props whether it be for a Horses Stamp Issue or perchance for the Orchid Stamp Issue ... why not use *Desert Orchid*, the champion horse, to open a Post Office on the Orchid Stamp Day.

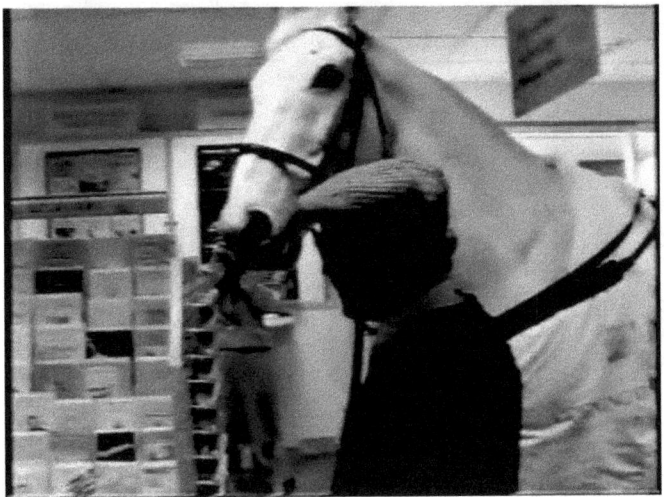

Yes, with horsebox parked behind Southend's New Post Office, officials from Post Office HQ asked if the horse would actually be coming into the post office as they had spent a great amount of money on the hard-wearing carpet … to which I said yes, for the publicity pictures.

But being a wise old PR operative, we had already done a deal with the trainer to walk *Desert Orchid* around a bit for him to do his business. Of course, it worked a treat – so he was clean and tidy for the press launch of the new Post Office ... not like the *Warhorse* Film Launch in London where no-one had thought about Mother Nature and had 'organic flow' on the red carpet !

Gardening expert, Peter Seabrooke, with Orchids for the stamp issue!

Also, on the animal theme – someone appears to be a little fearful, or doesn't like cats too much, at this Post Office opening! There was a successful formula for opening small rural post offices – giant cake, free booze, PA system and a local personality – on virtually ever occasion the entire village would turn out!

DIARY OF A PUBLICITY GURU

Over the years, animal costumes have been a good plus for media pictures – so much so, that almost every year of this 30-year transit has seen their use.

In the early 1970s it was Theatre Zoo, or Zoo Theatre, in London that had almost every animal costume. Based in deepest Covent Garden, my first collection of costumes for the summer-long carnival season gave me an early start to drive to London, when in those days it was quiet first thing and there were no peak traffic times.

Not so nowadays.

So, arriving in Covent Garden shortly after 9.00am, I was amazed both at the size of the shop and the array of costumes contained inside.

Gorillas, giraffes, lions, tigers, bears, horses, cows – you could name them all. They even stored a frog, seen here on leap year day at a Post Office opening in Suffolk – although, for a stills picture, the frog didn't have to leap in the silly season of August when news is thin on the ground!

Chapter 18
Creating Even More Media..........

Stamp Issues in the 1990s continued to be the bread and butter of media relations, marketing and promotions. They didn't cost that much and, with the wide variety of subject matter, there were numerous excuses to use a creative mind and obtain coverage.

Alice Through the Looking Glass!

The Scottish Stamps gave an excuse to serve haggis to customers – the catering manager of the time said there was not much difference between haggis and a *McDonalds*!

Some bagpipe music too!

The Antarctic team at Cambridge for the period of Travel Stamps.

The use of stamps alongside the official opening of a new branch in London.

Roman Stamps and a chariot to boot with a visit to local BBC studio.

DIARY OF A PUBLICITY GURU

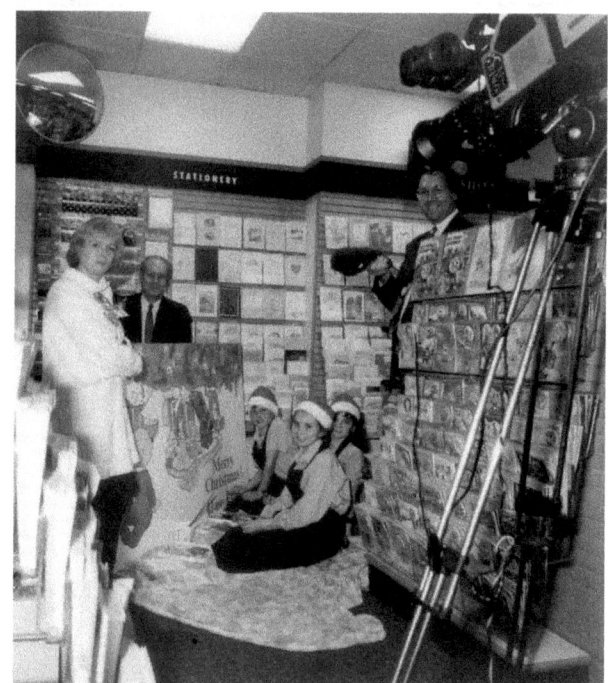

Christmas Stamps involving local school children painting a giant stamp.

DIARY OF A PUBLICITY GURU

I well remember one Christmas the stamps were designed by a Luton schoolgirl and a meeting to discuss TV launch coverage on *Blue Peter* took me to BBC TV in Shepherd's Bush. There I was to discuss filming with the then *Blue Peter* producer, Biddy Baxter.

Her office was busy with numerous staff, desks full of props and – here's one I made earlier! – and no meeting or conference room.

Biddy said she wanted to discuss the issues in private so she opened a cupboard, some two wardrobe doors, and we stood in the sort of V-shaped doorway with the doors wrapped around the two of us for the meeting – interesting top secret experience at the BBC!

Aircraft Stamps – and time to link up with the RAF – it seems every base has a 'Gate Guardian' in the form of an aircraft that was based there over the years – so a flying visit to RAF bases around the UK, again with great pix.

DIARY OF A PUBLICITY GURU

One stamp event became a bit of a problem. For the Swans stamps in 1993, we had a life-size swan created as a plaster-cast model – it looked so real – and it was moved around the country for local young dancers to perform *Swan Lake* to music inside post offices.

Following the week-long promotion, it was decided to donate the lovely swan to the Wetlands Trust at Welney. My calibre car of the time converted into a small estate car, so the swan was positioned over the fold-down rear seats in the back – alas, giving a view of the swan through the side windows.

Speeding along the now A14 from Bury St Edmunds, I was overtaken by a police car – and the officers saw the swan. It is, of course, illegal to move swans – they are Royal Property – but these young police officers felt I was moving a real swan and, with sirens going, they both indicated to me that I should pull over. Sadly, they were unaware of the lorry in front of them and watching me, they did not watch the lorry in front and they unfortunately collided into the back of it.

I continued my journey to Welney and was welcomed with the life-sized swan!

Towards the end of the 1990s and the turn of the century Father Time and the Millennium at the country's most easterly Post Office – Lowestoft – where they would meet the year 2000 first.

In all walks of life there is always someone who does something a bit different – and, for the *Guinness Book of Records*, there's a stamp-licking champion!

DIARY OF A PUBLICITY GURU

Costumes – so, over the years, my late colleague Michael Heath of MH Designs was a genius in publicity ideas, creating a wide-range of costumes and props to order ...

Gas Flame!

Postman Pat!

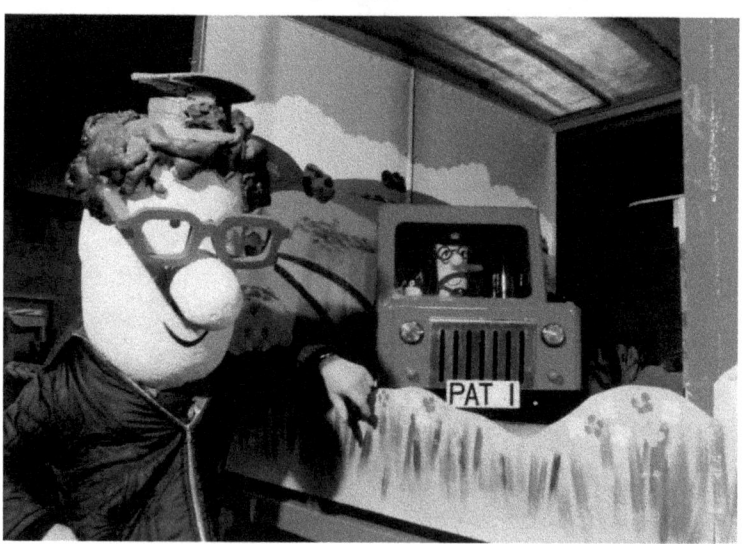

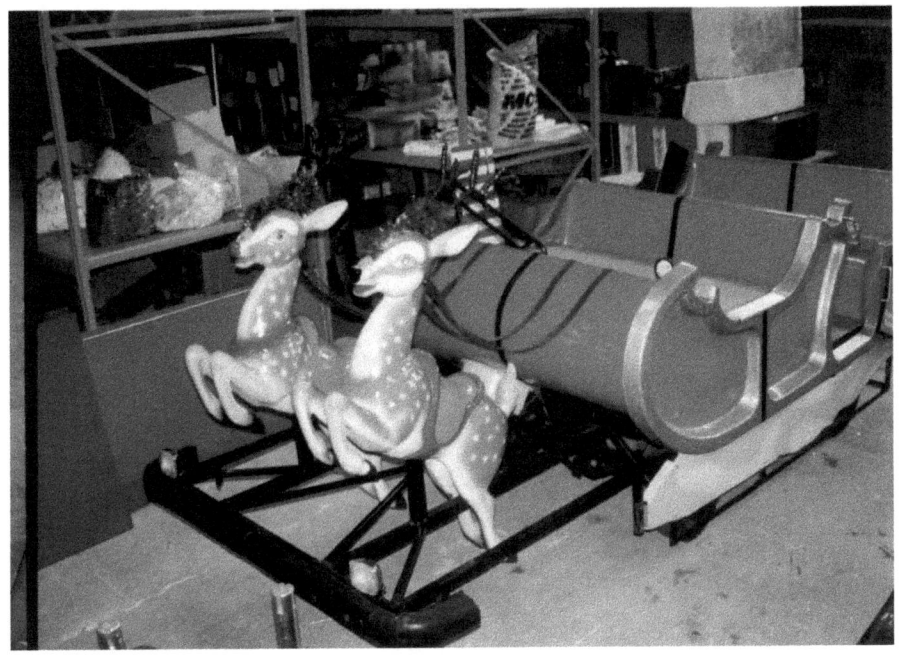

Santa Claus Sleigh!

Giant heart!

Money and Branding!

Giant stamps with a real Doctor!

And tickets for Blakey from 'On the Buses'!

The '90s was an era of giants – giant props, giant scissors, giant cakes!

A Post Office in a London Hairdressing Salon – the man in the centre starred in a hair shampoo commercial at the time – I wonder where Ray Nightingale is now? Think he has a top London salon! He was very nervous about the photocall !!

And a touch of religion always goes down well

*The personality scenario came into its own in the '90s.
Above: Sir Geoff Hurst, who scored the winning goal in the 1960s
World Cup for England with Football Stamps at Ipswich.*

Chapter 19
End of 20th Century Highlights

'Only Fools & Horses' star – the late Buster Merryfield – was good value at Luton, launching the 'Comic Relief' Lottery Scratchcards. I fed him a story that Del had given him a bit of money to make themselves Millionaires with the new lottery – the money came from the Post Office till and, of course, went back into the till afterwards!

Arthur Bostrum from ''Allo 'Allo!' launches Bureau de Change At Ipswich.

David Clements who produced children's programmes on BBC TV with the toy stamps.

BBC 'Songs of Praise' presenter Pam Rhodes, with Roger Harrison of Eurostar, opening a Post Office at Stevenage.

National weatherman, John Kettley, opening a rural post office and is presented with a tuppenny blue post office tie.

Yes Christmas and the Post Office gave so many possiblities – a journalists jolly to show off the Post office and its travel business – the E111 form for health insurance abroad, Bureau de Change etc etc.

Stamp designers finish off their designs!

And PR events such as a night at The Stables at Wolverton Milton Keynes for a concert with the late Johnnie Dankworth & Cleo Laine.

DIARY OF A PUBLICITY GURU

These were the '90s in PR, Publicity and Media!

With the opening of a major new Post Office in the City of Norwich – what better personality to use than Dame Barbara Windsor with an anniversary of her famous *Carry On* films?

The plan was a 1.30pm grand opening, fanfare, giant scissors, ribbons, etc, followed by a personal appearance at the local cinema and a screening of one of Barbara's best ever *Carry On* films – *Carry on Camping*. The schedule was that Barbara would be overnight at a Norwich hotel, then do a recce at Castle Mall for the opening ceremony, a pre-event lunch, then to Castle Mall for live TV coverage.

With all media in place – the press, the Beeb, ITV, local radio stations and even Hospital Radio – we were set to go on a massive media event.

Maybe there was some jealousy with another retailer in the Castle Mall Shopping Centre as the fire alarm went off (in Argos) and the complete centre was evacuated, putting live TV in a fix!

DIARY OF A PUBLICITY GURU

However, thirty minutes later we were all back for the event – making a story within a story, giving the media an even bigger story, thereby giving longer airtime. At that time, the Post Office was keen on evaluation of almost everything including media – resulting in this event giving over £1m worth of positive coverage. All good things, etc.

Another famous personality was part of the Colchester Post Office opening – yes, Darren Day – he was also a local boy. He had all the good fortune of *Summer Holiday* success alongside other musicals so, again, a prop – a London Transport bus. Hidden away at the back of the former Post Office and sorting office, complex discussions were made as to the official opening ceremony. Darren Day would arrive on a London bus to a fanfare and do the speech ... then we'd all be off down the hill for lunch. With traffic wardens at the ready, the double decker would have to go the wrong way along a single-track town centre road.

Strong branding, giant scissors – but media wanted a twist. They bribed the bus driver to drive off quickly – leaving Darren Day to chase, or almost miss, the bus. Great coverage of, once again, a story within a story.

DIARY OF A PUBLICITY GURU

Alongside the fun stories, you could always find the real humane story. On this occasion, a war memorial to colleagues who gave their lives in the First World War, had to be moved to a new building. But how do you move a War Memorial and hold a service of re-dedication?

Alas, no re-dedication service can occur unless the War Memorial has been damaged before, or during, its move. So, with the aid of a small hammer … the Royal British Legion then said we could hold a service. With the Bishop of Colchester and members of families who could relate to those mentioned in stone, the service was held, giving some really positive media coverage for the good old post office.

*Back to fun times – here's the late, very famous actress, Peggy Mount, taking a stab at our lovely giant cake.
A Trojan of an actress and good value too!*

DIARY OF A PUBLICITY GURU

And alongside the many 'greats' – here's a great prop. Taking a life-size dinosaur around the country gave added publicity with AA road reports on numerous radio stations – beware of a very large load travelling along the A and B such and such roads – the Post Office are moving their dinosaur to the next publicity location.

With the onetime TV 'great' Johnnie Morris, it was very good value. Meeting him at Norwich Railway Station, I asked why he had brought a suitcase – he opened it and said, "Sometimes these events go on a bit!" … inside was a crate of 12 cans of ale! The problem with the prop was that it had a very long tail and, manhandling the trailer, it gave my car a very prominent bonk and dent in the rear wing – but, winging it I did … Royal Mail Stamps paid for the repair.

The Radar stamps were a special for Bawdsey and Watson-Watt who invented the system. A visit to RAF Bawdsey and a trip on the Felixstowe Ferry across to Harwich by boat resulted in superb TV coverage for the Post Office, the RAF and Lifeboats – a really good joint exercise.

The man holding the stamp was involved with something that he told me about, which he referred to as 'the electronic highway'. A quiet man from Woodbridge, he said this was a very big invention ... it later became known as the Internet ... how right he was!

DIARY OF A PUBLICITY GURU

Above: One of the launch pictures with Post Office Counter's Boss, John Maine, covered in trophies and the now familiar sight ... a bottle of 'champoo'!

Oh, the days of self-esteem and promoting the organisation and saying how good we were! Best Post Office took the biscuit and, of course, both print and broadcast media filled endless pages and airtime with acres of coverage and important radio minutes, often turning to hours, of positive PR.

Left: Just one of the many local radio events – how many Best Post Offices can there be?

The lovely TV presenter and broadcaster, Paul Barnes, on yet another Best Post Office presentation. There were some business miles to be done here – with almost 18,000 Post Office branches in the UK – how many had to be visited?

A rather young-looking Steve Scrutton at BBC Essex, filling yet another studio with winners and runners-up. But, are these all finalists in a bigger competition?

Above: The lovely broadcaster and personality, Pam Rhodes, launching the national competition.

At the end of the day, the winner has to be presented by 'Tina Turner' to be *Simply the Best!*

DIARY OF A PUBLICITY GURU

As the '90s came to an end, and indeed the end of the century, what better way of making a mark in history than to create special diaries? These were designed to be housed in the Millennium Memory Bank with stamps and personal entries from far and wide, famous and infamous, those with rank and file and, indeed, just Joe Public. Whether or not these diaries ever got to the Millennium Memory Bank is questionable, but the media coverage was good.

During 30 years of turbulent times, there were massive changes in PR, media, marketing, fashion and technology – and, indeed, society itself. Here's the last ever lighthouse lamp keeper of all times as the system goes automatic.

Staying sometimes at the first ever Motor Hotel in Oxford – before 'Travelodges' – it's demolished now.

DIARY OF A PUBLICITY GURU

It's been an all-singing all-dancing 24/7 party of being a brand guardian!
Recognizing Chinese New Year or handling international media for the Diana Stamps.

(CBS Japanese Sat TV, BBC, ITV, CNN etc) or
visiting Switzerland Post Office PR Boss, Dick Sperio,
my first mobile (international) phone call … or the Batmobile!

Behind the scenes: 'Operation Gum Gum'.

In North London, a so-called charity were taking in and washing the postmark ink off stamps and re-selling them, making a £9 million revenue loss to the Post Office annually. In the garden of a house, under a tarpaulin, there were hundreds of stamps awaiting the wash. The pre-dawn raid resulted in many arrests and the girls turning up for work at 9.00am to do the laundry were also taken into custody.

A 3.00am start to the day with investigating officers, Police and Royal Mail detectives.

Above: Helen Shapiro at a school local to her in Dunmow.

Below: Star cricketer, Geoff Boycott, batting for the unveiling of the new sorting machines in Chelmsford.

Perchance a touch of travel – yes, a postmaster was called Dick Whittington and you could travel on the Post Office's underground railway (Mailrail) if you were a competition winner.

Or a meeting with the famous (late actress) Carmen Silvero of *'Allo 'Allo!* Fame.

Creating news coverage for TV en-route to Blenheim Palace to meet the Duke of Marlborough and his son Lord Rupert
... or producing a campaign with regional weatherman for a warm front of detector vans coming across the country.

DIARY OF A PUBLICITY GURU

*TV for Roses Stamps with the illustrator and designer ...
or taking journalists for a Bureau de Change event on 'Eurostar'
to Paris or Brussels ...*

DIARY OF A PUBLICITY GURU

It's been a plus 30-year whirl of playing to the media, being creative and writing endless media releases!

Announcing, introducing, entertaining and presenting ...

DIARY OF A PUBLICITY GURU

Behind the scene on a radio phone-in ...
or costume adjustments ...

Taking controls on the
Flying Postie ... or judging
'Write a Letter' competition ...

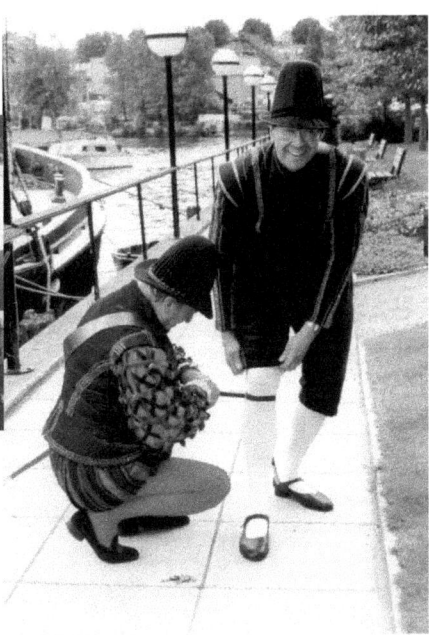

(right) broadcaster Christine Webber

(second from right) Sally Thomsett

DIARY OF A PUBLICITY GURU

Wearing a publicity Poco hat ... arranging TV interviews with BBC's Stewart White ...

Hosting good old conferences ... or watching time on-air ...

Setting the Christmas scene ... in the limelight with Darren Day ...

Or creating a stamp event ... sorting an air-flight ...

How it's all changed! In the early days of postcodes, they were used on road-signs … how far we have now come with sat-nav!

DIARY OF A PUBLICITY GURU

So, has Post Office PR helped the world?
Probably in many unknown ways …

It's cheered people up, educated everyone into postcode usage
and spent a lot of publicity money …
it's caused acres of newspaper coverage and days,
if not weeks or months, of airtime …

DIARY OF A PUBLICITY GURU

Sometimes a lonely existence ...

but, other times, fulfilling ...

and rewarding ...

The professional PR/Media Award from Mike Kay, Chairman of the Association of Travel Clubs UK ... and Christmas wishes in the office!

Journey to see Father Christmas 10,000 times over …

but hard work behind the scenes, often in very cold conditions …

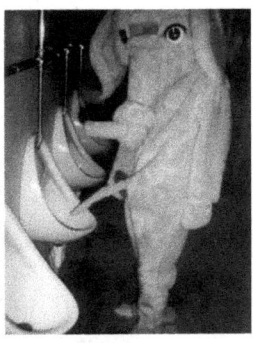

… a lasting memento of a stained-glass stamp at Ely Cathedral …

… props … costumes … and salvation!

DIARY OF A PUBLICITY GURU

Conferences – Brussels – Paris all part of the daily life!

Chapter 20
Thank you and Farewell ?

A life-time of 24/7 defending and promoting the post office does of course reflect on many memories. With my specialism of tv and radio, numerous newsworthy stunts were held for the regional, national and international tv stages. In the early days news coverage was put together on location by 16mm sep-mag film which had to be back in the studios for 14.30 in order to process cut and edit the footage for the 6.30 regional news programme. So life was full of morning pr events to get the story on-air that day which always involved DRs – despatch riders often booked at very late notice to whizz through the traffic back to the studios. On each and every tv event – the common phrases used were 'have you booked a dr' and if the item was not for the same day transmission or maybe not ever to be used it might be done under a 'strawberry filter' !! But in post office news terms I only heard this once in over 30 years !

While we said goodbye to the 'Gin & Tonic Man' early in this lifetime of pr, marketing, media and publicity, booze did not go away. For in the 1980s and 90s the mobile booze kit was key. A small black foldable case contained glasses, gin whisky, sherry and mixers. One Christmas a Royal Mail Director was to do a tour of sorting offices to check the Christmas Post and wanted to do it all by helicopter – he said, "And get a follow-up helicopter for the booze kit too !"

Life could be good in respect of 'jollies' British Air Ferries which became British World Airlines at Southend were responsible for many of the 'Flying Postie' operations both to the Channel Islands and internal flights – Southend, Norwich, Luton. Stansted, Liverpool Birmingham. Sometimes with only a few day's notice their Commercial Director Mike Kay would ring and ask if I would like to bring as few journalist friends for a day out in Guernsey or Jersey – breakfast over the channel, a vintage bus tour of the island, VIP lunch, duty-frees, and afternoon tea on the journey back to Southend.

'Would you like to join us for lunch in Switzerland tomorrow,' said Mike Kay. How can you refuse that ! A breakfast flight to Basle then lunch somewhere nice – yet on the return trip when you look through the windows of the aircraft and see 2 engines as it were 'feathering' and the pilot announces we are making an additional stop at Lydd Airport, and on landing two fire engines are travelling along the runway at the same speed as the aircraft – you wonder if there are easier ways to make a living!!

Presentation of a Penny Black Tie to Station Commander RAF Bruggen

Then one Saturday a VIP trip to an RAF base in Germany to do a Postman Pat stunt to the children of those stationed out there, or an inaugural flight of the new 146 aircraft of British World Airlines to Nice with lunch up in the mountains at a village called Eze – life could be great.

Then there was the trip to Clement Ferrand in France with not only VIP package all the way but a specially chartered train for a mountain journey then lunch up in the mountains in a snowy hotel.

But back to reality however - mid-way through this 'glitzy' career loads and loads of contacts were established. And Christmas Cards were an important part of the relationship along with goodie bags of stamps, pens and executive giveways – like this rather nice vintage van penholder.

One Christmas was extremely busy with the 'post early for Christmas' message and mid-November the Christmas cards were sorted. One of the PAs had put them into three piles – said she, "these are the ones you sign Paul Diggens, these are the ones you sign Paul and finally for your female contacts you sign these love from Paul.

Unbeknown to me over lunch-time someone knocked the 3 piles with their sandwich container but in the afternoon I got underway to sign the 200+ cards as instructed and off they went in the post.

On the pre-Christmas drinks rounds in tv and radio circles I was slightly amused when confronted by a number of male media contacts saying thanks for the Christmas Card signed love from Paul!!! – well you can't win em all !!

But to win over the media the props had to be larger than life – even the scissors could cut the opening giant tape !

THE TOYS!

But in the end the glitzy life cannot last forever – the post office felt times needed to change – was PR & Media a luxury they could not afford ? Interestingly my 25 year long service award did not happen. After a year or so I did ask if I would receive this award and at the time there was yet again a Post Office reorganization that came either just before Christmas or just before the school summer holidays so you always lived in awe as to whether you had a job in the future or even had to reapply for your job which I had to do on a number of occasions. When 28 year's service was achieved I did ask again and I was told that everything in that carrier bag in the corner of the office was mine! There was a watch that had a tatty strap and only worked for a few months, a cheapo pen that hardly worked and a certificate rubber-stamped by the then MD. The best thing of all was the frame. Interesting how a senior manager was dealt with – my neighbour British Gas man in a van had 2 new colour tvs for his 25 years service – giant one for lounge and smaller one for bedroom, new razor and he and his wife had a luxury weekend away in the country to celebrate. Wonder if the Post Office should learn some lessons ??

DIARY OF A PUBLICITY GURU

In the late 1980s and during the 1990s all of the media coverage from local regional and national newspapers, local and national radio and regional and national tv was monitored and apportioned a price of obtaining free editorial publicity on a positive or negative basis. I think tv for instance was charged at £20K a minute for positive publicity. So being interviewed for the 'Diana' stamps by local regional national and international crews plus world service generated over £12M worth of positive pr and publicity for the post office, the most anyone had achieved ever !

Despite all this, I was replaced by a Communications Officer – colleagues in tv in later years said it was a real laugh – 'Paul with you and your team we would get an immediate media question answer, with Communication Officers an answer within 3 days and by that time the story was dead' So the people that ran the post office from year 2000 did not know about the importance of public relations and publicity perchance !!

Bus Boys

Thank you, team ... wherever you are!

DIARY OF A PUBLICITY GURU

THE END ?

The End or perchance new beginnings………………………..

Behind the scenes Hospital Radio and Hospital tv have been a big part of my life. In order to promote hospital radio Colchester I introduced a real-live concept programme called Mersea Island Discs which later became Mersea Discs – if you were stranded on Mersea Island because of high tide across the causeway that links to the mainland, what records would you like to listen to on your car radio until the tide goes down and you are able to cross to the mainland again – a real live drama programme as on most days Mersea does become an island !

The programme ran for 500 editions bringing in local personalities, MPs Town Mayors, BBC's Miss Marple (Joan Hickson) and many many East Anglia personalities.

DIARY OF A PUBLICITY GURU

But included with the success of the programme came a black cloud from the BBC. The now late Roy Plomley had the idea of Desert Island Discs many years back and for the 400th edition for Mersea Island Discs we thought it would be an idea to invite Roy Plomley himself.

A strict letter came back saying – ' I am always happy to co-operate with hospital radio stations but I am surprised that I was not given the pleasure of granting my permission for a copy of my programme which has been broadcast now for a number of years !'

He pointed out the Hospital Radios station were not above the copyright laws !!

I did apologise to him but pointed out this is a real live situation of being stranded on an Essex island to which Roy Plomley responded to say that no copyright was really necessary but please give my programme Desert Island Discs a mention from time to time please !!!

Perchance you can win some !!!

Then it was from Hospital Radio to Hospital TV and for 21 years the service provided local-life programmes to Colchester and Clacton Hospitals and to 100 plus residential care homes in mid and north east Essex. The service folded as a charity when funding became unavailable around 2016 and the last programmes went out that Christmas. The idea was that a local company or firm would get a one minute commercial at the front end of the earlier two hour vhs programme tape and latterly the two hour dvd for sponsoring the programmes. There was lots of fun but hard work in producing four 2 hour programmes every year but over the life-time of CHTV some 640 programmes were produced now being uploads of the Colchesterhistorychannel on facebook.

Mayor of Colchester joins tv presenter Pam Rhodes for the launch of Colchester Hospital Television Service in 1993.

DIARY OF A PUBLICITY GURU

Most years the Christmas programmes were produced in June or July !

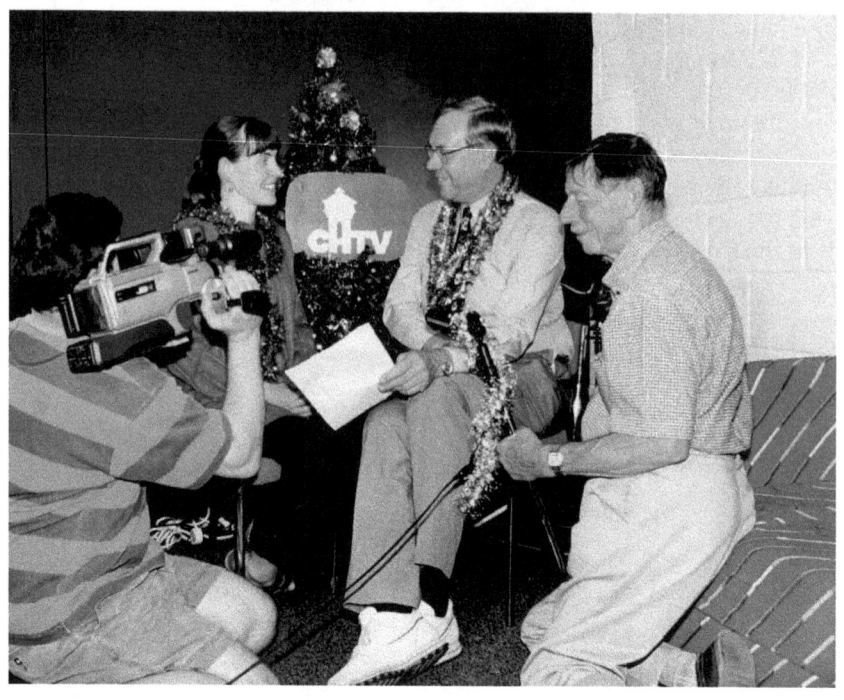

DIARY OF A PUBLICITY GURU

BROADCASTERS HAVE PRODUCED 600 PROGRAMMES

Hospital TV alive and well after 21 years on the airwaves

■ Celebrity launch – presenter Pam Rhodes launched the TV station with manager Paul Diggens

By CAROLINE TILLEY
caroline.tilley@nqo.com

IT has been 21 years since Colchester's hospitals got their own TV show.

Colchester Hospital TV went on air for the first time in October 1993, with television presenter Pam Rhodes, who anchored Anglia TV's evening news programme, launching the show.

It had started as an idea to extend hospital radio.

Mayor of Colchester Wesley Sanford asked hospital radio's programme controller Paul Diggens to look at a television service for Colchester's hospitals.

After six months of research and appeals for equipment, the station was launched.

Mr Diggins, station manager, said: "I remember giving our broadcast tapes to the League of Hospital Friends and they had to load them into a super VHS player in a cupboard in the operating theatre of Colchester District General Hospital.

"This was where the aerial cables and broadcast kit for the hospital was located."

CHTV went out to 40 TV screens in Colchester General and 20 in Clacton District Hospital. It has come a long way since

■ On air – cameraman Brian Lawrence, Jackie Andrews with Jack Hannibal

then. Programmes are now broadcast to residential care homes and sent to Essex Libraries Housebound Service – firstly with VHS tapes, but for the past few years with DVDs.

It makes four seasonal DVDs a year.

Mr Diggins said: "We have covered so much in 21 years.

"In the early days we covered football matches from Layer Road, the annual Oyster Feast in the Town Hall, the replacement of the North Station Railway Bridge over Christmas and the New Year and Jackins motorcade and shop in High Street, to the official opening of Colchester's New Post Office at the top of North Hill with showbusiness personality and local boy Darren Day.

"We also filmed significant events such as how the town and area were after the sudness of Princess Diana's death with an interview with the mayor signing the book of remembrance and the station flowers and messages ahead of the war memorial and the royal visit of the Queen to Harwich and Colchester.

Almost 600 programmes have been produced and broadcast in that time.

The autumn DVD will be sent out to more than 70 residential care homes in Essex.

It includes 50 years of Colchester history from Colchester Round Table, entertainment with Circus Tyanna, a vintage car rally and fireworks with King Cnut Knights display from the Castle Park.

Each member of the team was also interviewed and asked for their favourite clip down the years.

Moments chosen ranged from the royal train arriving at Harwich town station to filming at Butterfly Farm in Elmstead Market.

The TV station, which was jointly funded by King Coels Kittens and Colchester Catalyst Trust, has been helped by numerous local companies.

The 21 year celebratory programme is available on YouTube at the colchesterhospitaltv channel.

DIARY OF A PUBLICITY GURU

And awards were there too. The Association of Travel Trades Clubs invited me to Majorca one November just before Christmas. I could not get my head around the Christmas trimmings in the hotels and Christmas trees are the beach. However Mike Kay made it very worth my while with their award.

DIARY OF A PUBLICITY GURU

With tv my specialism in the post office the after PO life became one of film – the opportunity to film the last ever days of Hovercraft across the channel….

An executive goodbye video for Virgin Atlantic……..

And life on the railways route filming for many TOCs (train operating companies) with retail sales for rail enthusiasts all over the world from www.225studios.com – life is constantly busy even in retirement !

Footnote

The Post Office took me far and wide in travelling both in this country and in Switzerland, Holland, Northern Ireland and the Channel Islands. I always carried with me a Train Travel Warrant Book to write out at a moment's notice a ticket for any journey in the UK and there was even an Air Warrant Book for immediate air-travel tickets !

Motoring on post office business was a big part of the operation. Like my grandfather I was always interested in statistics and like him I logged all my mileage, petrol and costs from the days of my first car in November 1969. All these years later, and now on an all-electric car, in the petrol days until February 2020 I travelled 669,699 miles, using the earth's resources of 20,883 gallons, costing £46,383.29 – sorry world !!!

Lightning Source UK Ltd.
Milton Keynes UK
UKHW020758120522
402881UK00004B/187